I0430050

Taking Shelter From the Storm:

Building a Safe Room For Your Home or Small Business

Includes Construction Plans and Cost Estimates

FEMA P-320, Third Edition / August 2008

TEXAS TECH UNIVERSITY

Portland Cement Association

FEMA

NATIONAL
CONCRETE MASONRY
ASSOCIATION
Sustainable Concrete Products for Structures and Hardscapes

 Preface

Since the First Edition of FEMA 320, *Taking Shelter From the Storm: Building a Safe Room Inside Your House,* was printed in August 1998, nearly 600,000 copies of the publication have been released. Initiatives attributed to FEMA 320 have resulted in almost 20,000 residential safe rooms being constructed with federal funding assistance. Further, other initiatives since the publication was first released include tens of thousands of safe rooms being constructed with private funds to meet these protection criteria, the creation of the National Storm Shelter Association (NSSA) as a self-monitoring safe room and shelter governing body, and the development of a new consensus standard from the International Code Council® (ICC®) for the design and construction of storm shelters. The existence of this document, and the safe room designs provided herein, have helped to save the lives of thousands of individuals and families. FEMA is pleased to have this opportunity to update and improve the guidance through this new edition of FEMA 320, *Taking Shelter From the Storm: Building a Safe Room For Your Home or Small Business.*

Taking Shelter From the Storm:

Building a Safe Room For Your Home or Small Business

Table of Contents

 # Introduction

Every year, tornadoes, hurricanes, and other extreme windstorms injure and kill people, and cause millions of dollars worth of property damage in the United States. Even so, more and more people build homes in tornado- and hurricane-prone areas, possibly putting themselves into the path of such storms.

Having a safe room built for your home or small business can help provide "near-absolute protection" for you and your family or employees from injury or death caused by the dangerous forces of extreme winds. Near-absolute protection means that, based on our current knowledge of tornadoes and hurricanes, the occupants of a safe room built according to this guidance will have a very high probability of being protected from injury or death. Our knowledge of tornadoes and hurricanes is based on substantial meteorological records as well as extensive investigations of damage to buildings from extreme winds. It can also relieve some of the anxiety created by the threat of an oncoming tornado or hurricane. All information contained in this publication is applicable to safe rooms for use in homes as well as in small businesses.

Should you consider building a safe room in your home or small business to provide near-absolute protection for you, your family, or employees during a tornado or hurricane? The answer depends on your answers to many questions, including:

- Do you live in a high-risk area?
- How quickly can you reach safe shelter during extreme winds?
- What level of safety do you want to provide?
- What is the cost of a safe room?

This publication will help you answer these and other questions so you can decide how best to provide near-absolute protection for you and your family or employees. It includes the results of research that has been underway for more than 30 years, by Texas Tech University's Wind Science and Engineering (WISE; formerly known as the Wind Engineering Research Center or WERC) Research Center and other wind engineering research facilities, on the effects of extreme winds on buildings.

This publication provides safe room designs that will show you and your builder/contractor how to construct a safe room for your home or small business. Design options include safe rooms located underneath, in the basement, in the garage, or in an interior room of a new home or small business. Other options also provide guidance on how to modify an existing home or small business to add a safe room in one of these areas. These safe rooms are designed to provide near-absolute protection for you, your family, or employees from the extreme winds expected during tornadoes and hurricanes and from flying debris, such as wood studs, that tornadoes and hurricanes usually create.

TORNADO OCCURRENCE AND RESULTANT LOSSES ARE INCREASING

In 1950, the National Weather Service (NWS) started keeping organized records of tornadoes occurring in the United States (U.S.). Since that time, 1953 was the deadliest year (519 deaths). The average in recent years has been 62 deaths per year. Deaths caused by tornadoes were 38, 67, and 81 for 2005, 2006, and 2007, respectively. As of May of this year, 110 deaths have been caused by tornadoes.

In addition to deaths, tornadoes cause injuries and devastating losses of personal property. Insurance claim losses from a single tornadic event of $1 billion and higher are becoming more frequent. So far in 2008, tornadoes

This photograph from FEMA's photo library shows the vivid reality of how lives are impacted by tornadoes.
(Lafayette, TN – February 5, 2000)

SOURCE: JOCELYN AUGUSTINO/FEMA

have resulted in insured losses of more than $1 billion (almost $850 million of which from the mid-South outbreaks on February 5 and 6; in March, Atlanta and its surrounding counties were struck by a tornado that caused $349 million in losses).

Although hurricanes and earthquakes generally generate higher losses per event, since 1953, tornadoes (and related weather events) have caused an average of 57 percent of all U.S. insured catastrophic losses. In 2007, that number increased to 69 percent.

SOURCE: A.M. BEST, CNN

In August 2008, the International Code Council® (ICC®), with the support of the National Storm Shelter Association (NSSA), released a consensus standard on the design and construction of storm shelters. This standard, the *ICC/NSSA Standard for the Design and Construction of Storm Shelters* (ICC-500), codifies much of the extreme-wind shelter recommendations of the early editions of FEMA 320 and FEMA 361, *Design and Construction Guidance for Community Safe Rooms* (first edition, July 2000). FEMA 361 contains detailed guidance for the design and construction of community safe rooms, which also provide near-absolute protection, the level of protection provided in the residential safe rooms of this publication. The ICC-500 provides the minimum design and construction requirements for extreme-wind storm shelters and is expected to be incorporated into the 2009 International Building Code® (IBC®) and International Residential Code® (IRC®). It is important that those involved in the design, construction, and maintenance of storm shelters be knowledgeable of both FEMA guidance and ICC standards that pertain to sheltering from extreme winds.

The safe room designs presented in this publication meet or exceed all tornado and hurricane design criteria of the ICC-500 for both the tornado and hurricane hazards.

The National Association of Home Builders (NAHB) Research Center has evaluated these designs for construction methods, materials, and costs for the earlier editions of this publication. Engineers at Texas Tech University, engineering consultants, and FEMA have confirmed the design requirements for the expected forces from wind pressure and the impact of typical flying debris. When installation and foundation requirements are addressed by a local design professional, these designs will meet or exceed the design requirements set forth in the ICC-500 for residential and small community shelters (less than 16 persons) for both tornado or hurricane hazards. The safe rooms in this publication have been designed with life safety as the primary consideration.

Section I: Understanding the Hazards

Almost every state in the United States has been affected by extreme windstorms such as tornadoes and hurricanes. Virtually every state has been affected by a "considerable" tornado (see the terms in Figure I-1). All Atlantic and Gulf of Mexico coastal areas in the United States – including coastal areas of Puerto Rico and the U.S. Virgin Islands – and coastal areas of Hawaii have been affected by hurricanes. Even in states not normally considered to be susceptible to extreme windstorms, there are areas that experience dangerous extreme winds. These areas are typically near mountain ranges, and include the Pacific Northwest coast.

What Is a Tornado?

According to the American Meteorological Society's *Glossary of Meteorology*, a tornado is "a violently rotating column of air, pendant from a cumuliform cloud or underneath a cumuliform cloud, and often (but not always) visible as a funnel cloud." Tornadoes typically occur in the spring and summer months, but can occur at any time in any part of the country. Tornadoes are sometimes spawned by hurricanes. The severity of a tornado is categorized by the Enhanced Fujita Scale (EF Scale). As of February 2007, the EF Scale (see Figure I-1) was adopted by the National Oceanic and Atmospheric Administration (NOAA) to replace the Fujita Scale (F Scale). The EF Scale is designed similar to the F Scale, but has been revised to have a greater number of Damage Indicators, which are used to characterize the degree of damage experienced by buildings during a tornado.

Not all parts of each state are at equal risk from tornadoes. For example, while Texas has the highest number of recorded tornadoes, the state's least tornado-prone area (along the Gulf coast) has been hit by fewer tornadoes than northeastern Arkansas. Comparing the numbers of tornadoes recorded in different areas within a state can give you a better understanding of potential tornado activity in those areas. Figure I-2 shows the summary of recorded EF3, EF4, and EF5 tornadoes per 2,470 square miles in the United States and its possessions and territories. Between 1950 and 2006, tornadoes caused 5,506 deaths and 93,287 injuries.

DEFINITION

In this publication, the term **missiles** refers to debris and other objects picked up by the wind and moved with enough force to damage and even penetrate windows, doors, walls, and other parts of a building. In general, the stronger the wind, the larger and heavier the missiles it can carry and the greater the risk of severe damage or injury. But even small stones, branches, and other lighter missiles can easily break glass doors and windows.

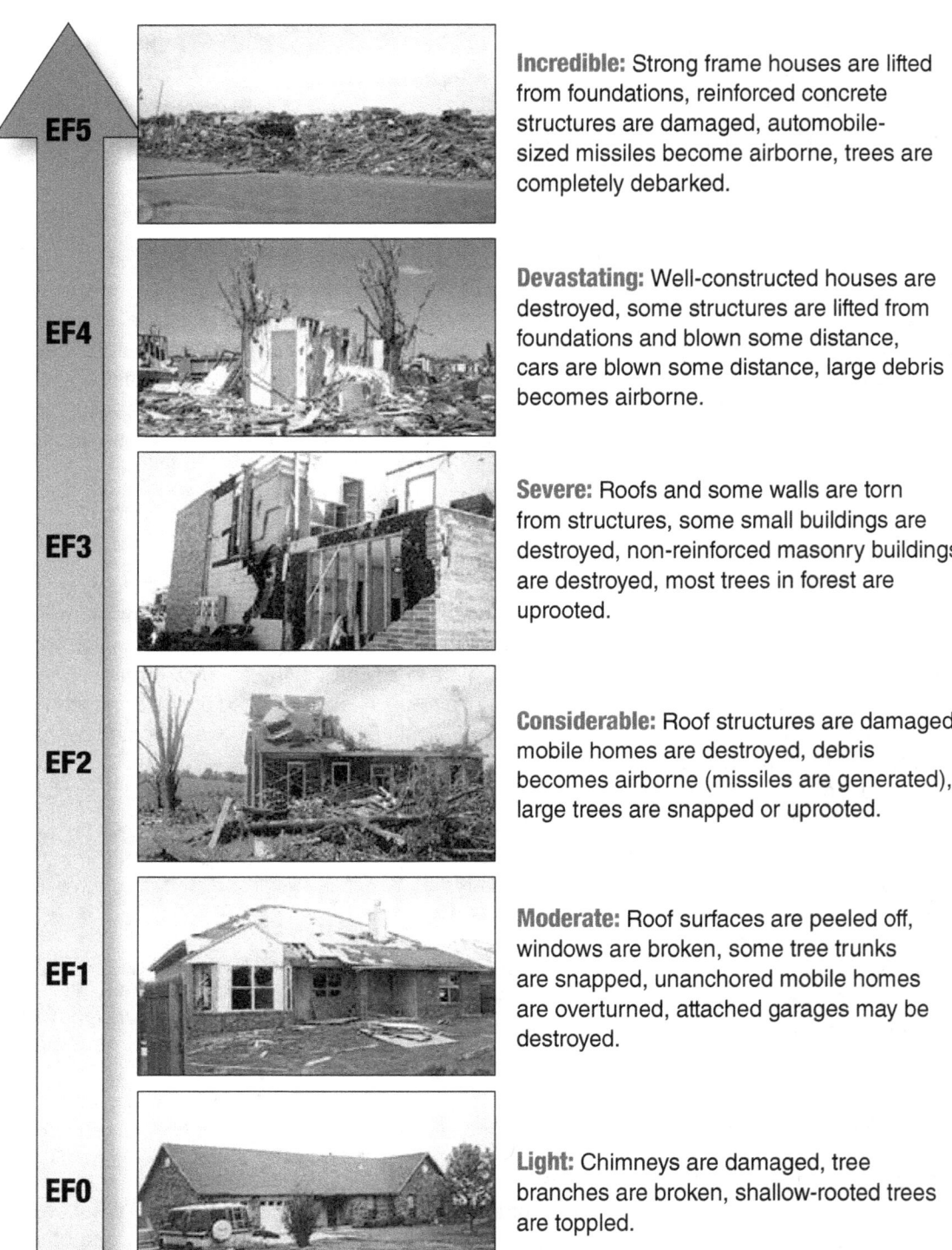

EF5

Incredible: Strong frame houses are lifted from foundations, reinforced concrete structures are damaged, automobile-sized missiles become airborne, trees are completely debarked.

EF4

Devastating: Well-constructed houses are destroyed, some structures are lifted from foundations and blown some distance, cars are blown some distance, large debris becomes airborne.

EF3

Severe: Roofs and some walls are torn from structures, some small buildings are destroyed, non-reinforced masonry buildings are destroyed, most trees in forest are uprooted.

EF2

Considerable: Roof structures are damaged, mobile homes are destroyed, debris becomes airborne (missiles are generated), large trees are snapped or uprooted.

EF1

Moderate: Roof surfaces are peeled off, windows are broken, some tree trunks are snapped, unanchored mobile homes are overturned, attached garages may be destroyed.

EF0

Light: Chimneys are damaged, tree branches are broken, shallow-rooted trees are toppled.

Figure I-1. Typical tornado damage

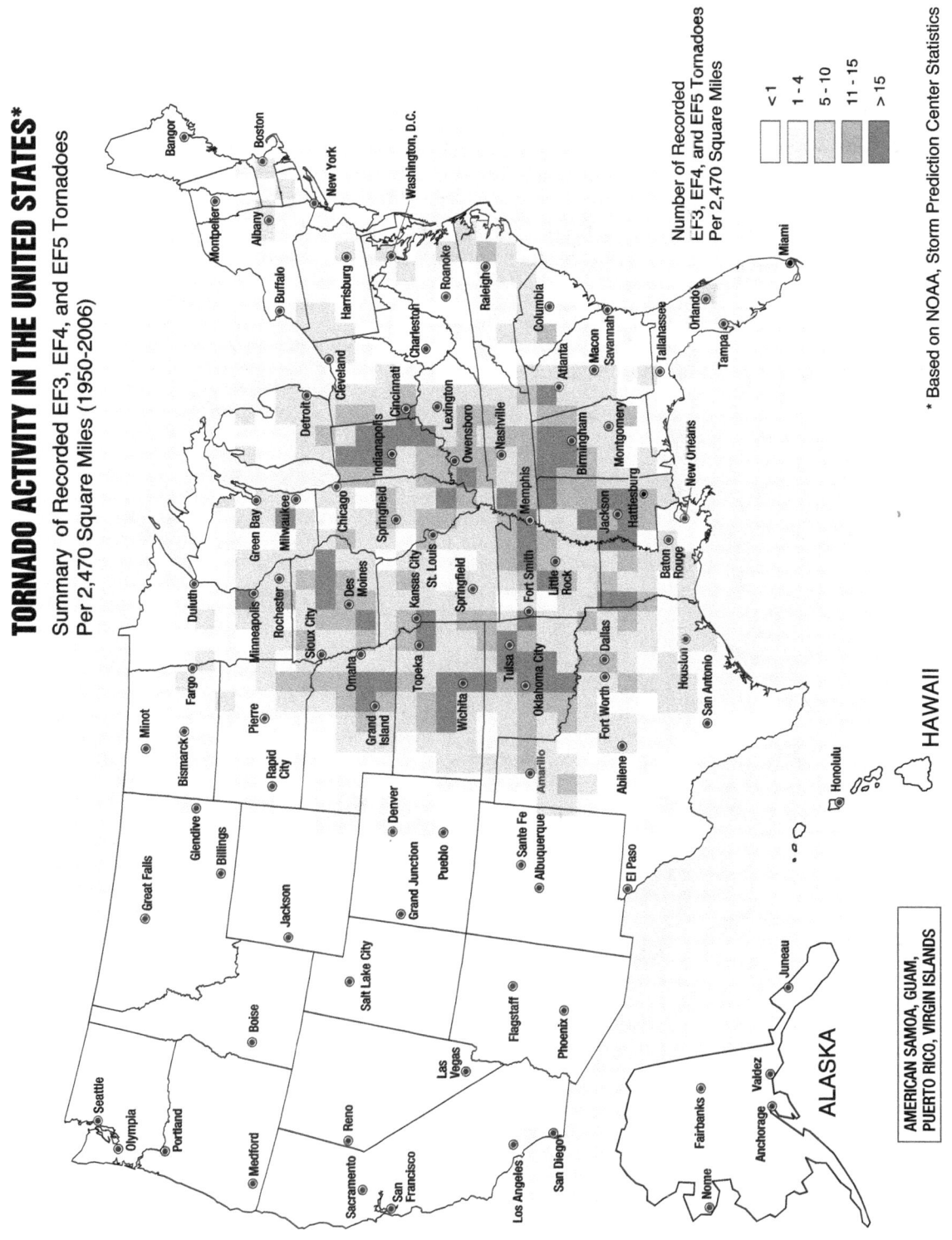

TORNADO ACTIVITY IN THE UNITED STATES*
Summary of Recorded EF3, EF4, and EF5 Tornadoes Per 2,470 Square Miles (1950-2006)

Number of Recorded EF3, EF4, and EF5 Tornadoes Per 2,470 Square Miles

- <1
- 1 - 4
- 5 - 10
- 11 - 15
- >15

* Based on NOAA, Storm Prediction Center Statistics

HAWAII

ALASKA

AMERICAN SAMOA, GUAM, PUERTO RICO, VIRGIN ISLANDS

Figure I-2. The number of tornadoes recorded per 2,470 square miles

What Is a Hurricane?

Hurricanes are categorized by the Saffir-Simpson scale (see Figure I-3).

In the United States, 279 hurricanes were recorded to have made landfall between 1851 and 2006. Over one-third of these hurricanes (96) were classified as major hurricanes (designated Category 3 and higher on the Saffir-Simpson Hurricane Scale). Hurricanes have made landfall in Florida more than in any other state. The second most hurricane-affected state is Texas, but every state on the Gulf coast and bordering the Atlantic Ocean is susceptible to damage caused by hurricanes, as are U.S. island possessions and territories. Hurricanes between 1900 and 2006 resulted in 17,832 deaths.

In recent years, the U.S. territories of Puerto Rico, American Samoa, and Guam have been seriously affected by numerous tropical cyclones.

Catastrophic: Roof damage is considerable and widespread, window and door damage is severe, there are extensive glass failures, some complete buildings fail.

Extreme: Extensive damage is done to roofs, windows, and doors; roof systems on small buildings completely fail; some curtain walls fail.

Extensive: Large trees are toppled, some structural damage is done to roofs, mobile homes are destroyed, structural damage is done to small homes and utility buildings.

Moderate: Some trees are toppled, some roof coverings are damaged, major damage is done to mobile homes.

Minimal: Damage is done primarily to shrubbery and trees, unanchored mobile homes are damaged, some signs are damaged, no real damage is done to structures.

Figure I-3. Typical hurricane damage

Do You Need a Safe Room?

On the basis of 60 years of tornado history and more than 150 years of hurricane history, the United States has been divided into four zones that geographically reflect the number and strength of extreme windstorms. Figure I-4 shows these four zones. Zone IV has experienced the most and the strongest tornado activity. Zone III has experienced significant tornado activity and includes coastal areas that are susceptible to hurricanes. The release of the ICC-500 has codified much of FEMA's guidance for safe room design and construction. However, there are additional details in the ICC-500 regarding hurricane shelters, including a new shelter design wind speed map that could be helpful to understanding your risk of extreme-wind events due to hurricanes. A safe room designed and constructed to the prescriptive designs included in this publication (and properly sited to address flood hazards) will meet or exceed the ICC-500 residential and small community shelter (less than 16 people) design criteria.

A safe room using the prescriptive designs of this publication should not be installed in a hurricane-prone area that may be inundated by storm surge from any hurricane, including Category 5 hurricanes. Further, it is best not to install residential or small community safe rooms in any area susceptible to flooding defined by the 500-year floodplain. However, in areas not prone to storm surge, a safe room may be installed within mapped floodplains only when the designs provided herein:

- Are accepted as meeting the safe room elevation flood criteria presented in the text box on pages 23 and 24
- Comply with all local floodplain ordinances
- Are coordinated with local emergency management

Your home or place of business is probably built in accordance with local building codes that consider the effects of minimum, "code-approved" design winds for your area. Building codes require that buildings be able to withstand a *design* wind event. In most tornado-prone regions, the building code design wind event is a wind event with 90 mph winds. For hurricane-prone areas, design wind events in the code range from 90 to 150 mph. A tornado or extreme hurricane can cause winds much greater than those on which local code requirements are based. Having a home built to "code" does not mean that your home can withstand wind from any event, no matter how extreme. The safe room designs in this publication provide a place to seek safe shelter during these extreme-wind events.

A safe room may be designed and constructed to meet all applicable FEMA criteria. However, use of the safe room during a hurricane may not be in compliance with mandatory evacuation orders of the local jurisdiction. FEMA recommends that all safe room occupants comply with local jurisdictional directions and orders during a hurricane event (which may include evacuation) even if they have constructed a safe room.

The worksheet on page 10 will help you determine your level of risk from these extreme events and will assist you in your consideration of a safe room. If you decide that you need a safe room, Section II will help you and your builder/contractor in planning your safe room. To learn more about the wind history for the area where you live, check with your local building official, meteorologist, emergency management official, or television weather reporter.

WIND ZONES IN THE UNITED STATES*

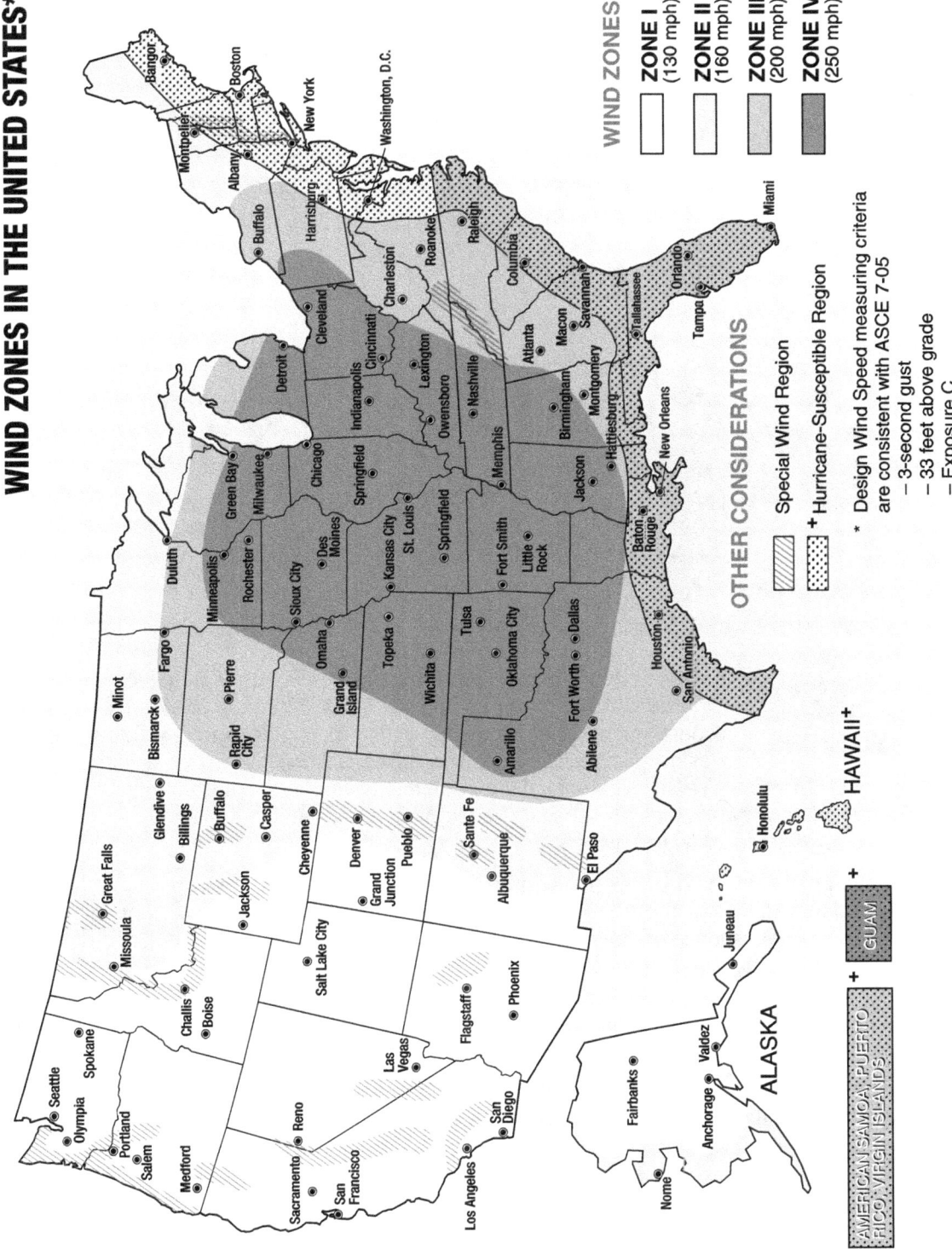

WIND ZONES

- **ZONE I** (130 mph)
- **ZONE II** (160 mph)
- **ZONE III** (200 mph)
- **ZONE IV** (250 mph)

OTHER CONSIDERATIONS

- Special Wind Region
- + Hurricane-Susceptible Region

* Design Wind Speed measuring criteria are consistent with ASCE 7-05
 – 3-second gust
 – 33 feet above grade
 – Exposure C

Figure I-4. Wind zones in the United States

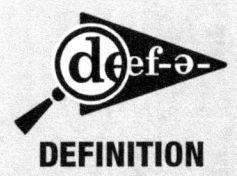
In this publication, the term **storm surge** means an abnormal rise in sea level accompanying a hurricane or other intense storm, and whose height is the difference between the observed level of the sea surface and the level that would have occurred in the absence of the cyclone. Storm surge (see Figure I-5) is usually estimated by subtracting the normal or astronomic high tide from the observed storm tide.

DEFINITION

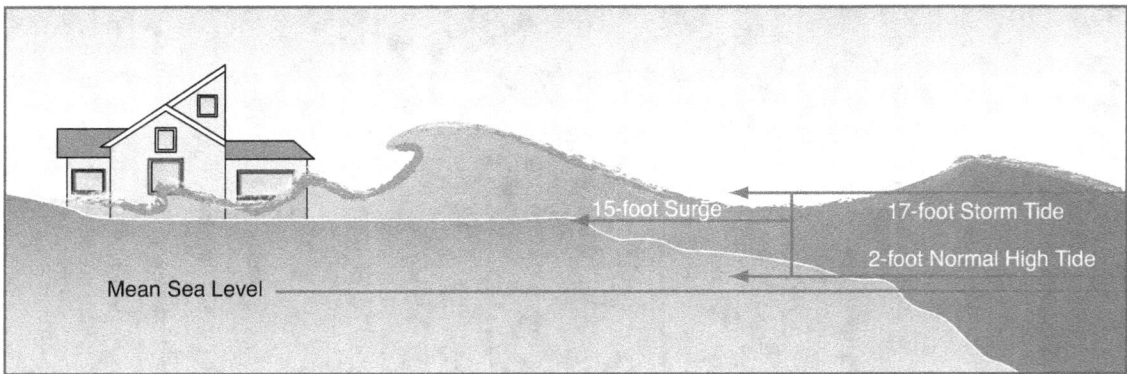

Figure I-5. Storm surge

WARNING

A safe room designed to protect you and your family or employees from a hurricane or tornado should not be built in an area expected to be flooded during a hurricane, thunderstorm, or other severe weather event. Residents of hazard-prone coastal areas should abide by the warnings of their local emergency services personnel and evacuate to safer ground. The protection from wind provided by safe rooms and shelters is quickly negated when people find themselves trapped and inundated by floodwaters.

If you do not know whether your home or small business is in a **storm surge** area or other area subject to flooding, check the community service section of your local phone book for storm surge evacuation information or ask your local emergency management or floodplain management official.

Homeowner's Worksheet: Assessing Your Risk

To complete the worksheet on page 10, refer to the tornado occurrence and wind hazard maps for tornadoes and hurricanes on pages 3 and 7 (Figures I-2 and I-4, respectively). Using the map on page 3, note how many tornadoes were recorded per 2,470 square miles for the area where you live. Find the row on the worksheet that matches that number. Next, look at the map on page 7 and note the wind zone (I, II, III, or IV) in which you live. Find the matching column on the worksheet. Finally, find the box inside the worksheet that lines up with both the number of tornadoes per

2,470 square miles in your area and your wind zone. The color of that box tells you the level of your risk from extreme winds and helps you decide whether to build a safe room.

Hurricane-susceptible regions can be seen in Figure I-4, running from the southern tip of Texas to the Northeast. Revised hurricane shelter design wind speeds have been released in the ICC-500. For the purpose of the prescriptive solutions offered in this publication, the wind speeds given in Figure I-4 are used to calculate pressures and required resistances for residential safe rooms.

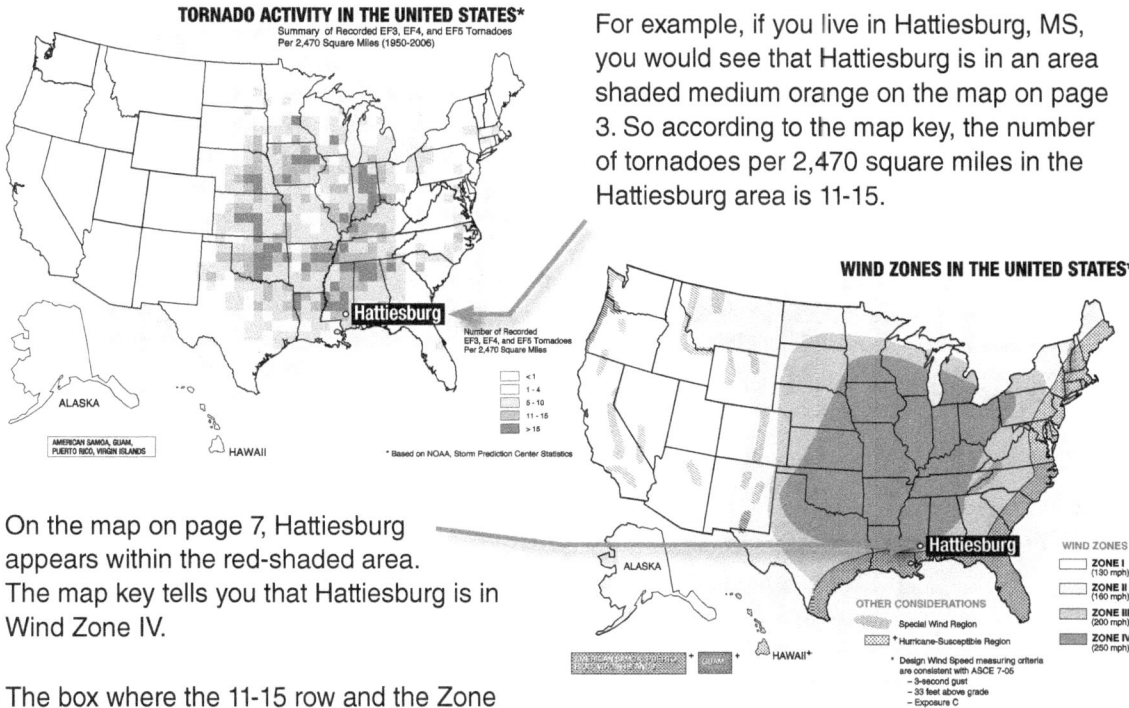

TORNADO ACTIVITY IN THE UNITED STATES*
Summary of Recorded EF3, EF4, and EF5 Tornadoes Per 2,470 Square Miles (1950-2006)

For example, if you live in Hattiesburg, MS, you would see that Hattiesburg is in an area shaded medium orange on the map on page 3. So according to the map key, the number of tornadoes per 2,470 square miles in the Hattiesburg area is 11-15.

On the map on page 7, Hattiesburg appears within the red-shaded area. The map key tells you that Hattiesburg is in Wind Zone IV.

The box where the 11-15 row and the Zone IV column meet is shaded dark blue, which shows that you live in an area of high risk. A safe room is the preferred method of wind protection in high-risk areas. Note that some areas of low or moderate risk, shown as pale blue or medium blue in the worksheet, are within the region of the United States that is subject to hurricanes (see Figure I-4). If you live in this hurricane-susceptible region, your risk is considered high, even though the worksheet indicates only a moderate or low risk.

		WIND ZONE (SEE FIGURE I-4)			
		I	**II**	**III**	**IV**
NUMBER OF TORNADOES PER 2,470 SQUARE MILES (SEE FIGURE I-2)	**< 1**	LOW RISK	LOW RISK ★	LOW RISK ★	MODERATE RISK
	1 – 4	LOW RISK	MODERATE RISK ★	HIGH RISK	HIGH RISK
	5 – 10	LOW RISK	MODERATE RISK ★	HIGH RISK	HIGH RISK
	11 – 15	HIGH RISK	HIGH RISK	HIGH RISK	HIGH RISK
	> 15	HIGH RISK	HIGH RISK	HIGH RISK	HIGH RISK

Table I-1. Homeowner's Worksheet

		WIND ZONE (SEE FIGURE I-4)			
		I	**II**	**III**	**IV**
NUMBER OF TORNADOES PER 2,470 SQUARE MILES (SEE FIGURE I-2)	**< 1**	LOW RISK	LOW RISK ★	LOW RISK ★	MODERATE RISK
	1 – 4	LOW RISK	MODERATE RISK ★	HIGH RISK	HIGH RISK
	5 – 10	LOW RISK	MODERATE RISK ★	HIGH RISK	HIGH RISK
	11 – 15	HIGH RISK	HIGH RISK	HIGH RISK	HIGH RISK
	> 15	HIGH RISK	HIGH RISK	HIGH RISK	HIGH RISK

LOW RISK	Need for an extreme-wind safe room is a matter of homeowner or small business owner preference.
MODERATE RISK	Safe room should be considered for protection from extreme winds.
HIGH RISK	Safe room is the preferred method of protection from extreme winds.
	Safe room is the preferred method of protection from extreme winds if the home or small business is in a hurricane-susceptible region.

Emergency Planning and Emergency Supply Kit

Whether or not you decide that you need a safe room in your home or small business, you can take two important steps to provide near-absolute protection for you, your family, or employees during a hurricane or tornado: prepare an emergency plan and put an emergency supply kit together. If you decide to build a safe room, your emergency plan should include notifying local emergency managers, first responders (local fire stations), and family members or others outside the immediate area that you have a safe room. This will allow emergency personnel to quickly free you if the exit from your safe room becomes blocked by debris. You should also prepare an emergency supply kit and either keep it in your safe room or be ready to bring it with you if you need to evacuate your home. Some of the items that the emergency supply kit should include are:

■ An adequate supply of water for each person in your home or small business (1 gallon per person per day)

■ Non-perishable foods that do not have to be prepared or cooked (if these include canned goods, remember to bring a manual can opener)

- ■ Disposable eating utensils, plates, cups, paper towels, etc.
- ■ A first-aid kit, including necessary prescription medicines, bandages, and antibiotic ointment
- ■ Tools and supplies:
  - flashlight (one per person; do not bring candles or anything that lights with a flame)
  - battery-operated radio or television and NOAA[1] weather radio
  - cellular phone or Citizen's Band (CB) radio
  - extra batteries for the above tools
  - wrench (to turn off gas and water)
  - insect repellent and sunscreen
  - personal hygiene items such as hand wipes and toilet paper
- ■ Extra change of clothing per person (store in plastic trash bags to keep clean and dry)
- ■ Appropriate outer wear (e.g., sunglasses, ponchos, jackets, gloves, headwear, boots, etc.)
- ■ Bedding materials such as pillows and blankets or sleeping bags
- ■ Special items for:
  - babies – formula, diapers, bottles, powdered milk
  - children – entertainment items such as books, games, or toys
  - adults – contact lenses and supplies, extra glasses, and a sufficient supply of prescription medications
  - pets – appropriate supplies such as water (1/2 gallon per day), food, leash, ID tag, carrying container, etc.
- ■ Additional items:
  - important documents such as insurance documents, a list of all your important contacts (e.g., family, doctors, insurance agents), banking information, leases/mortgage, proof of occupancy (such as a utility bill), and a waterproof container in which to keep these documents
  - ABC[2] rated fire extinguisher
  - roofing tarps or plastic sheeting
  - roll of large heavy-duty trash bags and duct tape
  - money (cash)

---

1 The National Oceanic and Atmospheric Administration (NOAA) Weather Radio (NWR) is a nationwide network of radio stations broadcasting continuous weather information directly from a nearby National Weather Service (NWS) office. NWR broadcasts NWS warnings, watches, forecasts, and other hazard information 24 hours a day, as well as post-event information for all types of hazards, both natural and technological. NOAA Weather Radios are available at electronics stores across the country and range in cost from $25 up to $100 or more, depending on the quality of the receiver and number of features. The NWS does not endorse any particular make or model of receiver.

2 ABC refers to fires originating from three types of sources: A - paper, wood, or fabric; B - gasoline or oil; or C - electrical.

You can get more information about emergency planning from American Red Cross (ARC) and FEMA publications, which you can obtain free of charge by calling FEMA at 1-800-480-2520, or by writing to FEMA, P.O. Box 2012, Jessup, MD 20794-2012. These publications include the following:

Planning Documents:

Are You Ready? An In-depth Guide to Citizen Preparedness, FEMA IS-22

Emergency Preparedness Checklist, FEMA L-154 (ARC 4471)

Emergency Food and Water Supplies, ARC 5055

Your Family Disaster Supplies Kit, ARC 4463

Preparing for Disasters for People with Special Needs, FEMA 476 (ARC 4497)

Safe Room Documents:

Design and Construction Guidance for Community Safe Rooms, FEMA 361

Safe Room and Community Shelter Resource CD, FEMA 388 CD

Tornado Protection - Selecting Refuge Areas in Buildings, FEMA 431

These publications are also available on the FEMA web site – http://www.fema.gov – and at the American Red Cross web site – http://www.redcross.org.

The Department of Homeland Security (DHS), has developed the READY.gov web site. You can find emergency planning and preparation guidance for all types of potential hazards. To obtain a copy of *Preparing Makes Sense. Get Ready Now,* go to http://www.ready.gov.

Section II: Planning Your Safe Room

Now that you better understand your risk from a tornado or hurricane, you can work with your builder/contractor to build a safe room to provide near-absolute protection for you, your family, or employees from these extreme windstorms. This section describes how extreme winds can damage a building, explains the basis of the safe room designs presented in this publication, and shows where you can build a safe room in your home or small business.

Building Damage

Extreme winds can cause several kinds of damage to a building. To understand what happens when extreme winds strike, you must first understand that tornado and hurricane winds are not constant. Wind speeds, even in these extreme-wind events, rapidly increase and decrease. An obstruction, such as a home, in the path of the wind causes the wind to change direction. This change in wind direction increases pressure on parts of the home. The combination of increased pressures and fluctuating wind speeds creates stress on the home that frequently causes connections between building components to fail.

For example, the roof covering, roof deck, or wall siding can be pulled off and the windows can be pushed into or suctioned out of a building. Figure II-1 shows how extreme winds can affect a building and helps explain why these winds cause buildings to fail. When wind is allowed to enter a building through a broken window, door, or roof section, that wind will act on the inside of a building much like air will act when forced into a balloon; it will push (or pull) on the walls and roof of the building from the inside. These forces within the building, added to the wind forces that are still acting on the outside of a building, often result in failure of the building because it was not designed to resist the forces acting on both the inside and the outside of the building

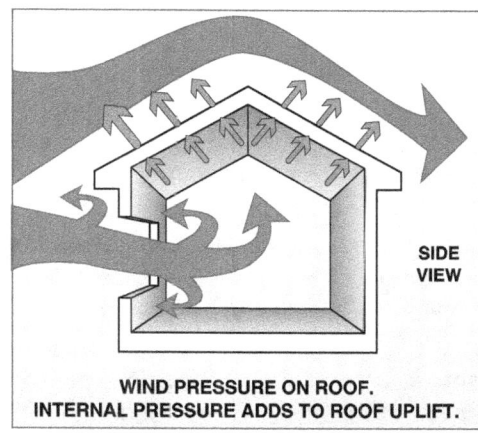

SIDE VIEW

WIND PRESSURE ON ROOF. INTERNAL PRESSURE ADDS TO ROOF UPLIFT.

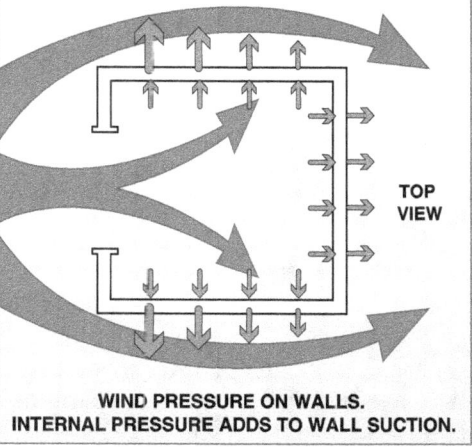

TOP VIEW

WIND PRESSURE ON WALLS. INTERNAL PRESSURE ADDS TO WALL SUCTION.

Figure II-1. Effect of extreme winds on building roof and walls

Buildings that fail under the effects of extreme winds often appear to have exploded, giving rise to the misconception that the damage is caused by unequal atmospheric or wind pressures inside and outside the building. This misconception has led to the myth that, during an extreme-wind event, the windows and doors in a building should be opened to equalize the pressure. In fact, opening a window or door allows wind to enter a building and increases the risk of building failure.

2" x 6" missile penetrating a refrigerator, midwest tornadoes of May 3, 1999

Damage can also be caused by flying debris (referred to as windborne missiles). If wind speeds are extreme enough, missiles can be thrown at a building with enough force to penetrate or perforate windows, walls, or the roof. For example, an object such as a 2" x 4" wood stud weighing 15 pounds, when carried by a 250-mph wind, can have a horizontal speed of 100 mph, which is enough force to penetrate or perforate most common building materials used in homes today. Even a reinforced masonry wall, which typically has hollow cells between reinforced cells, will be perforated unless it has been designed and constructed to resist debris impact during extreme winds. Because missiles can severely damage and even perforate windows, walls, and roofs, they threaten not only buildings but the occupants as well.

Palm tree pierced by plywood missile, Hurricane Andrew

DEFINITION

In this publication, missiles may be said to **penetrate** but not **perforate** the walls or roof of a safe room. For example, if a missile **penetrates** an exterior element of the safe room, this means the missile broke or damaged the exterior surface, but has not entered the safe room protected area. It is quite common for smaller missiles such as small stones, branches, and other lighter missiles to penetrate or imbed themselves into the exterior of the safe room and this is acceptable. However, the safe room walls, roof, and protected openings must not allow a missile to **perforate** these systems and allow the missile to enter into the safe room. When any portion of the safe room exterior is damaged such that a missile, or portion thereof, enters the protected area, the safe room exterior has been perforated and this is not acceptable.

Basis of Safe Room Design

The purpose of a safe room is to provide a space where you, your family, or employees can survive a tornado or hurricane with little or no injury. For tornado-prone areas, you should locate your safe room so that you can reach it as quickly as possibly from all parts of your home or business. In hurricane-prone areas, the safe room should not be built where it can be flooded during a hurricane. Your safe room should be readily accessible from all parts of your home or small business and should be free of clutter. To provide near-absolute protection for the occupants during extreme windstorms, the safe room must be adequately anchored to the home's foundation to resist overturning and uplift. The connections between all parts of the safe room must be strong enough to resist failure, and the walls, roof, and door must resist perforation by windborne missiles.

Missile (debris) launcher, Wind Engineering Research Center (WERC), Texas Tech University

Extensive testing by Texas Tech University and other wind engineering research facilities has shown that walls, ceilings, and doors commonly used in building construction to meet minimum building code requirements for standard building construction cannot withstand the impact of missiles carried by extreme winds. The safe room designs in this publication account for these findings by specifying building materials and combinations of building materials that will resist perforation by missiles in extreme winds.

2" x 4" wood stud launched at 100 mph pierces unreinforced masonry wall, WERC, Texas Tech University

Most homes, even new ones constructed according to current building codes, do not provide adequate protection for occupants seeking life-safety protection from tornadoes. Homes built to the modern building codes in hurricane-prone areas, such as windborne debris regions better resist wind forces and windborne debris impacts from hurricanes. However, a tornado or hurricane can cause wind and windborne debris loads on a home or small business that are much greater than those on which building code requirements are based. Only specially designed and constructed safe rooms, which are voluntarily built above the minimum code requirements of the IBC and IRC to the criteria of this publication, FEMA 361, or the ICC-500, offer life-safety occupant protection during a tornado or strong hurricane. The prescriptive designs provided in this publication provide near-absolute protection from winds and windborne debris associated with tornadoes or hurricanes.

NOTE

This publication provides FEMA safe room designs that meet or exceed the minimum shelter design requirements from the ICC-500 Storm Shelter Standard. The safe room designs in this publication are applicable for both tornado and hurricane hazards for the residential shelter and small community shelter (<16 occupants) design criteria identified in the ICC-500. The safe room design wind speed used is 250 mph and it has been designed as a "partially enclosed building" per ASCE 7 so as to meet the requirements of both residential and community safe rooms for tornado and hurricane hazards. Further, the missile resistance is based upon the 15-lb 2"x4" board missile traveling horizontally at 100 mph (again, the most restrictive criteria for both tornado and hurricane hazards). For additional design criteria and information for residential safe rooms, see the notes on the safe room plans in this publication and the design requirements for residential safe rooms in Chapter 3 of FEMA 361, *Design and Construction Guidance for Community Safe Rooms.*

The safe room designs provided in this publication are based on wind speeds that are rarely exceeded in the United States. Therefore, a safe room built according to these designs is expected to withstand the forces imposed on it by extreme winds without failing; this statement applies to both materials and connections used within the safe room. The intent of the designs is not to produce a safe room that will always remain completely undamaged, but rather a safe room that will enable its occupants to survive an extreme windstorm with minor or no injuries.

It is very important to note that predicting the exact strength of tornadoes and hurricanes is impossible. That is another reason why the safe room designs in this publication are based on extreme-wind speeds and why the primary consideration is life safety.

Designing a building, or portion of a building, to resist damage from more than one natural hazard requires different, sometimes competing, approaches. For example, building a structure on an elevated foundation to raise it above expected flood levels can increase its vulnerability to wind and seismic damage. These design approaches need to be thoroughly considered. In flood-prone areas, careful attention should be given to the warning time, velocity, depth, and duration of floodwaters. These flooding characteristics can have a significant bearing on the design and possibly even the viability of a safe room. Your local building official or licensed professional engineer or architect can provide you with information about other natural hazards that affect your area and can also recommend appropriate designs.

Safe Room Size

The amount of floor area per person that your safe room must provide depends partly on the type of windstorm from which the safe room is intended to protect you. Tornadoes are not long-lasting storms, so if you are relying on your safe room only for tornado protection, you will not need to stay in the safe room for as long a timeframe as you would for a hurricane. As a result, comfort is not of great concern, and a safe room that provides at least 5 square feet of floor area per person (note that wheelchair and bedridden occupants will require more space) will be big enough. This allocation of space per occupant also meets the minimum sizing requirements set forth in the ICC-500 for residential and small community tornado shelters.

When the safe room is intended to provide near-absolute protection from storms such as hurricanes, which can last for 24 hours or more, the comfort of the occupants should be considered. For this type of safe room, the recommended amount of floor area per person (standing or seated, not wheelchair or bedridden) varies from 7 to 20 square feet, depending upon the classification of the safe room. The minimum sizing requirement set forth in the ICC-500 for residential hurricane shelters is 7 square feet per occupant, while for small community shelters 20 square feet per occupant is specified. Necessities, such as water and toilet facilities, should also be provided in the small community safe rooms to maintain compliance with the FEMA 361 criteria and ICC-500 requirements. The safe room designs in this guide may have a minimum floor area of 48 square feet and a wall length of 6 feet. A safe room of that size used for hurricane protection could accommodate up to six people in reasonable comfort while maintaining compliance with the FEMA 361 criteria and ICC-500 requirements. The maximum floor dimensions in the safe room designs provided in this guide are shown to be 14 feet by 14 feet square, providing 196 square feet of safe room space. This amount of space could provide safe room protection for nine occupants at the ICC-500 square footage requirements for a small community hurricane shelter. If you plan to build a safe room with any wall longer than 14 feet, or with a wall height greater than 8 feet, consult a licensed professional engineer or architect.

NOTE

The safe room designs in this publication are applicable for any on-site construction. However, in a modular home, the safe room location would be limited to the basement or the below-ground module unless a separate foundation was designed and installed for the safe room. A modular home is a home constructed of modular units that have been built elsewhere, brought to the site, and installed on a permanent foundation.

NOTE

Consult FEMA 361 or the ICC-500 for guidelines and requirements on how to identify the net usable floor space for a safe room design from the publication if it is to be used as a small community safe room. Hard fixtures (sinks, bathtubs, etc.) and furnishings reduce the square footage within a safe room that is available for protecting occupants.

Foundation Types

Homes and other buildings vary in construction type as well as foundation type. Buildings constructed may have heavy walls systems, such as masonry or concrete, or they may have light walls systems constructed from wood framing, metal stud framing, or structural insulated panels (SIPs). Regardless of the structure above, the following types of foundations may be suitable for the installation of a safe room:

- Basement
- Slab-on-grade
- Crawlspace or pile (however, prescriptive solutions for pile foundations are not provided in the drawings included in this publication)

Basement Foundation Applications

A home on a basement foundation (see Figure II-2) is usually built on a foundation constructed of cast-in-place concrete or concrete masonry units (CMUs). Most concrete foundations are reinforced with steel bars or straps, but many CMU foundation walls have no steel reinforcement. The framing for the floor above the basement is supported by the exterior foundation walls and sometimes by a center beam.

Figure II-2.
Cross-section: typical basement foundation, with safe room

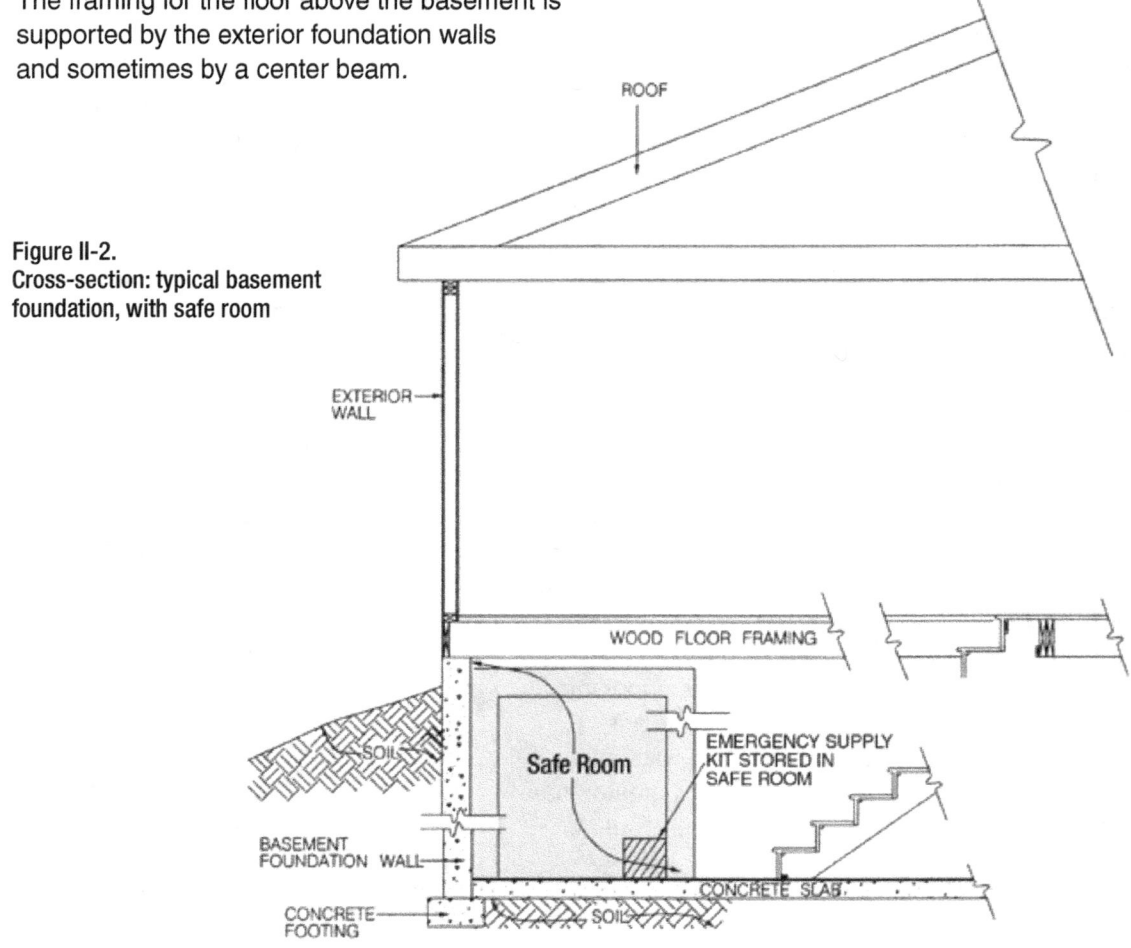

In a new or existing home with a basement, the safe room should be built in the basement. You can build the safe room as an entirely separate structure with its own walls, or you can use one or more of the basement walls as walls of the safe room. If you use the existing basement walls, they will have to be specially reinforced. Typical reinforcement techniques used in residential basement walls will not provide sufficient protection from missiles and resistance to extreme-wind loads. In new construction, your builder/contractor can reinforce the walls near the safe room during the construction of your home. Reinforcing the basement walls of an existing home is not practical.

The likelihood of missiles entering the basement is lower than for above-ground areas; however, there is a significant chance that missiles or falling debris will enter the basement through an opening left when a window, a door, or the first floor above has been torn off by extreme winds. Therefore, your basement safe room must have its own reinforced ceiling; the basement ceiling (the first floor above) cannot be used as the ceiling of the safe room. The safe room designs provided have considered that large, heavy loading from debris may be experienced by the safe rooms when a surrounding structure may collapse during an extreme-wind event. The roof decks of these safe rooms are designed to limit the damage that may be induced from these debris sources. Although the building may collapse around the safe room, it is still appropriate to install the safe room in the basement.

The least expensive type of safe room that can be built in a basement is a lean-to safe room, which is built in the corner of the basement and uses two basement walls. The lean-to safe room uses the fewest materials, requires the least amount of labor, and can be built more quickly than other types of basement safe rooms (see drawings B-01 and B-02).

In general, it is easier to add a basement safe room during the construction of a new home than to retrofit the basement of an existing home. If you plan to add a basement safe room as a retrofitting project, keep the following points in mind:

- You must be able to clear out an area of the basement large enough for the safe room.

- Unless the exterior basement walls contain steel reinforcement as shown on the design drawings provided with this publication, these walls cannot be used as safe room walls since they are not reinforced to resist damage from missiles and uplift from extreme winds.

- Exterior basement walls that are used as safe room walls must not contain windows, doors, or other openings in the area providing protection.

- The safe room must be built with its own ceiling, so that the occupants will be protected from missiles and falling debris.

Slab-on-Grade Applications

A slab-on-grade home or commercial building (see Figure II-3) is built on a concrete slab that is installed on compacted or natural soil. The concrete may be reinforced with steel that helps prevent cracking and bending. If you are building a new slab-on-grade home and want to install a safe room (of any material or type), it is recommended that the slab or foundation beneath the safe room wall be reinforced and thicker to ensure proper support and resistance to all loads (gravity and wind loads). The thickened slab will act as a footing beneath the walls of the safe room to provide structural support. It will also help anchor the safe room so that it will stay in place during an extreme-wind event, even if the rest of the home is destroyed.

In an existing home, removing part of the slab and replacing it with a thickened section to support a safe room would involve extensive effort and disruption inside the home. Some safe room designs presented in the drawings will require a footing to be placed due to the weight of the safe room itself, but others may be secured to an existing slab provided it has reinforcing steel in the concrete. Therefore, building a safe room with concrete or concrete masonry walls in an existing slab-on-grade home may not be practical unless the existing slab can be shown to have reinforcement adequate to support the safe room. If reinforcement can be shown to be present, the designs provided in these plans may be retrofitted to certain reinforced slabs. Similarly, a wood-frame safe room may be constructed atop an existing, reinforced slab because its walls are not as heavy and do not require the support of a thickened slab; however, these lighter safe room designs are vulnerable to displacement by wind loads. A wood-frame safe room can be created from an existing room, such as a bathroom or closet, or built as a new room in an open area in the home, such as a garage. Whenever an existing slab is used as the foundation for a safe room, a structural engineer should evaluate the adequacy of the slab to resist the wind loads acting on the safe room.

You can also build a safe room as an addition to the outside of a slab-on-grade home. This type of safe room must not only have proper footings, but also a watertight roof. Because a safe room built as an outside addition will be more susceptible to the impact of missiles, it should not be built of wood framing alone. Instead, it should be built of concrete or concrete masonry. Access to this type of safe room can be provided through an existing window or door in an exterior wall of the home.

In general, it is easier to add a safe room during the construction of a new slab-on-grade home than to retrofit an existing slab-on-grade home. If you plan to add a safe room to a slab-on-grade home as a retrofitting project, keep the following points in mind:

- The walls of the safe room must be completely separate from the structure of the home. Keeping the walls separate makes it possible for the safe room to remain standing even if portions of the home around it are destroyed by extreme winds.

- If you are creating your safe room by modifying a bathroom, closet, or other interior room with wood-frame walls, the existing walls and ceiling must be retrofitted or replaced with walls and a ceiling resistant to the impact of windborne missiles and other effects of extreme winds. In most cases, this means removing the sheathing, such as drywall or plaster, on either the inside, outside, or both sides of the walls and ceiling. Where possible, it is recommended that the shelter be built as a "new room" within the existing room in order to isolate the shelter from the home structure.

- If you intend to build a safe room with concrete or concrete masonry walls, a section of your existing slab floor may have to be removed and replaced with a thicker slab. As noted above, if this is necessary it may mean the retrofit may not be practical in the existing home.

Figure II-3.
Cross-section: typical slab-on-grade foundation,
with safe room

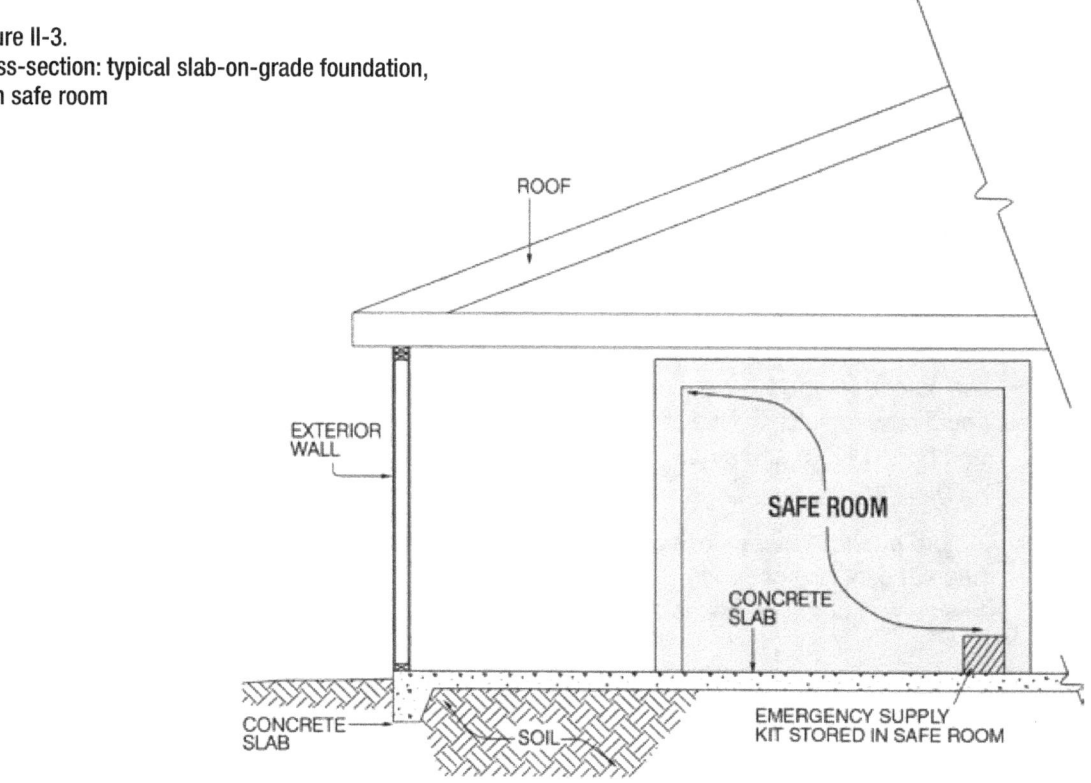

Crawlspace or Pile Applications

A home built on a crawlspace (see Figure II-4) usually has a floor constructed of wood framing. Along its perimeter, the floor is supported by the exterior foundation walls. The interior part of the floor is supported by beams that rest on a foundation wall or individual piers. Crawlspace foundation walls may be concrete, but are usually constructed from blocks of concrete masonry unit (CMU). They are often unreinforced and therefore provide little resistance to the stresses caused by extreme winds.

Building a safe room inside a home on a crawlspace foundation is more difficult than building a shelter inside a home on a basement or slab-on-grade foundation. The main reason is that the entire safe room, including its floor, must be separate from the framing of the home or the entire floor system and foundation of the home will be required to be constructed to support the extreme-wind loads acting on the safe room. In Figure II-4, a safe room is built inside the home or commercial building without using the floor system of the structure itself. In this option, the safe room has a separate concrete slab floor installed on top of earth fill and must be supported by steel reinforced concrete or CMU foundation walls. The floor system may be designed as open and elevated, but that design option is difficult to develop a prescriptive solution for and therefore is not provided in this publication. An alternative approach, which may be more economical, is to build an exterior safe room on a slab-on-grade foundation adjacent to an outside wall of the home and provide access through a door installed in that wall.

Ventilation in the area below the floor of the home is also an important issue. The wood-framed floor of a home on a crawlspace foundation is typically held 18 to 30 inches above the ground by the foundation walls for compliance with the building code. The space below the floor is designed to allow air to flow through so that the floor framing will not become too damp. It is important that the installation of the safe room not block this air flow.

In general, it is much easier to build a safe room inside a new crawlspace home than in an existing crawlspace home. If you plan to add a safe room to an existing crawlspace home as a retrofitting project, keep the following points in mind:

■ The safe room must have a separate foundation. Building the foundation inside the home would require cutting out a section of the existing floor and installing new foundation members, fill dirt, and a new slab – a complicated and expensive operation that is often not practical.

■ A more practical and more economical approach would be to build an exterior safe room, made of concrete or concrete masonry, on a slab-on-grade foundation adjacent to an outside wall of the home, as described above.

Figure II-4.
Cross-section: typical crawlspace foundation, with safe room

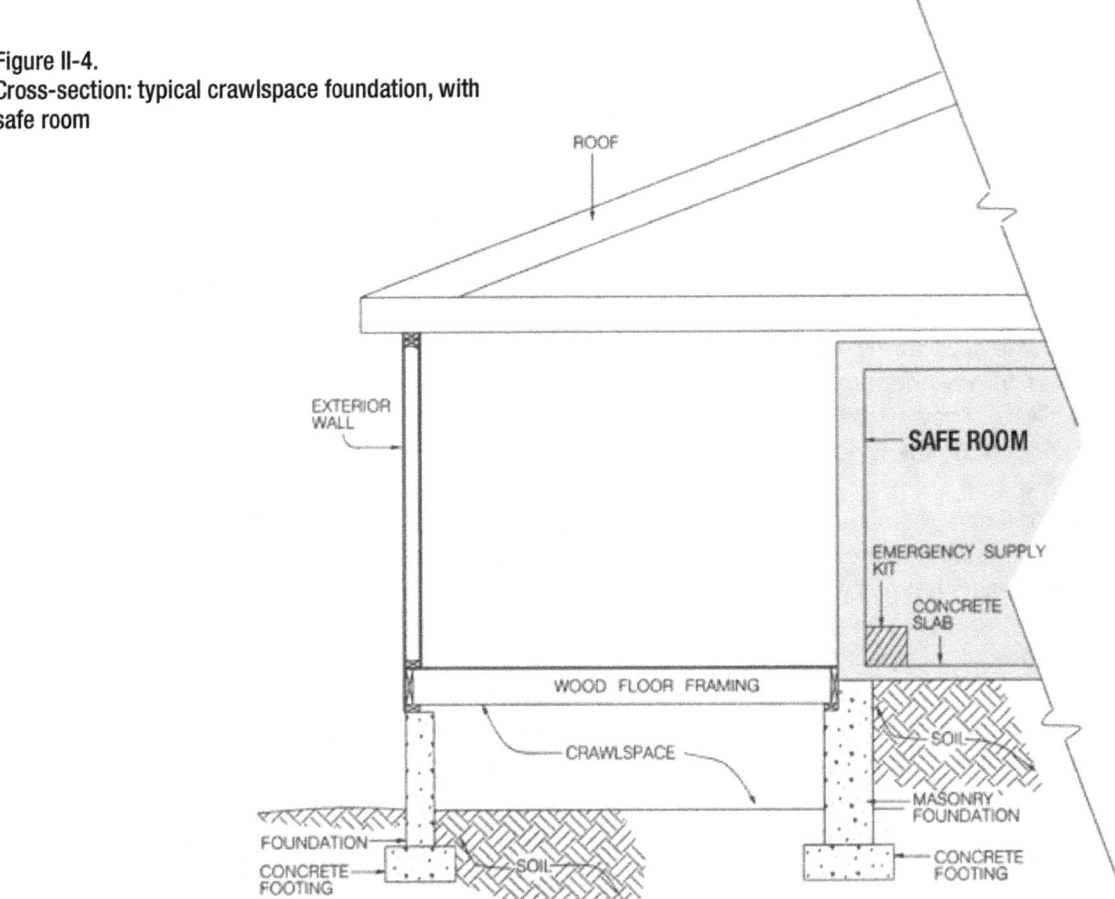

⚠ WARNING It is also important to remember that FEMA does not support placing safe rooms offering protection against extreme-wind events where floodwaters have the potential to endanger occupants within the safe room. Although the ICC-500 allows the placement of residential shelters in areas subject to flooding, FEMA safe room design criteria for residential safe rooms significantly limit the placement of safe rooms in Special Flood Hazard Areas (SFHAs). A residential safe room may only be sited in mapped SFHA where no wave action or high-velocity water flow is anticipated. Therefore, the installation of a safe room in a home supported by piles, piers, or columns should be scrutinized for its location with respect to flood hazards. With building connectors commercially available, it is extremely difficult to economically and structurally separate the safe room from the elevated floor framing and ensure that the safe room will withstand the forces of extreme winds.

If your safe room is located where coastal or riverine flooding may occur during hurricanes, it should not be occupied during a hurricane. Further, a residential safe room should not be located in an area subject to storm surge inundation. Although occupying such a safe room during a tornado may be acceptable, provided that the safe room is located where it will not be flooded by rains associated with other storm and tornado events, it should not be used during a hurricane. A residential safe room sited in the SFHA should meet the flood-specific FEMA safe room design criteria listed below. Consult your local building official or local National Flood Insurance Program (NFIP) representative to determine whether your home or small business, or a proposed stand-alone safe room site, is susceptible to coastal or riverine flooding. In any case, the installation of any safe room in a hurricane-prone area should be coordinated with local emergency management and law enforcement to ensure that its use during extreme-wind events is not a violation of any local or state evacuation plan.

Certain safe room designs provided in this publication may be elevated several feet above existing grade (see drawing sheets for specific details). However, even though the safe room floor may be elevated, it should be located *outside* of the following high-risk flood hazard areas:

1. The Coastal High Hazard Area (VE zones) or other areas known to be subject to high-velocity wave action; or

2. Areas seaward of the Limit of Moderate Wave Action (LiMWA) where mapped, also referred to as the Coastal A Zone in ASCE 24-05; or

3. Floodways; or

4. Areas subject to coastal storm surge inundation associated with a Category 5 hurricane (where applicable, these areas should be mapped areas studied by the U.S. Army Corps of Engineers (USACE), NOAA, or other qualified sources).

WARNING (CONTINUED)

If it is not possible to install or place a residential safe room outside the SFHA, the residential safe room may be placed in an area that has been determined by detailed study to be in an A, shaded X, or unshaded X Zone, but still outside of the high hazard areas identified above. In the instances when a residential safe room is needed in these flood-prone areas, the top of the elevated floor of the safe room should be elevated to the highest of the elevations specified below (see the appropriate Flood Insurance Study (FIS) or Flood Insurance Rate Map (FIRM)):

1. The minimum elevation of the lowest floor required by the floodplain ordinance of the community (if such ordinance exists); or

2. Two feet above the base flood elevation (BFE); i.e., 2 feet above the flood elevation having a 1 percent annual chance of being equaled or exceeded in any given year (100-year event); or

3. The stillwater flood elevation associated with the 0.2 percent annual chance of being equaled or exceeded in any given year (500-year event).

Residential Tornado Safe Room Exception: Where a residential tornado safe room is located outside of the hurricane-prone region as identified on Figure 3-2 of FEMA 361, and the community participates in the NFIP, the safe room need only be elevated to the minimum lowest floor elevation identified by the floodplain ordinance of the community.

Note, when installing a residential safe room in an area that has not been mapped or studied as part of a NFIP flood study (or equivalent flood study), the top of the safe room floor should be elevated such that it is 2 feet above the flood elevation corresponding to the highest recorded flood elevation in the area that has not been evaluated. Should no historical flood elevation data be available for the area, the elevation of the safe room floor should be set at the elevation identified by the local authority having jurisdiction.

In areas where Category 5 storm surges are not mapped, references in this publication to "Category 5" storm surge inundation areas should be taken to mean the area inundated by the highest storm surge category mapped.

New vs. Existing Homes or Buildings

The safe room designs in this publication were developed primarily for use in new homes or buildings, but some can be used in existing buildings. When a new home is being built, the builder/contractor can construct walls, foundations, and other parts of the home as required to accommodate the safe room. Modifying the walls or foundation of an existing home as necessary for the construction of a safe room is more difficult. As a result, some of the safe room designs in this publication are not practical for existing homes. Constructing a safe room within your home or small business puts it as close as possible to your family and/or employees. A safe room may be installed during the initial construction of a home or retrofitted afterward. As long as the design and construction requirements and guidance are followed, the same level of near-absolute protection is provided by either type of safe room. The following sections discuss these issues further. Also, for this discussion, the term "retrofit" refers to the process of making changes to an existing building.

It is relatively easy and cost-effective to add a safe room when first building your home or small business. For example, when the home is constructed with exterior walls made from CMUs (also commonly known as "concrete block;" see Figure II-5), the near-absolute protection level in FEMA 320 can be achieved by slightly modifying the exterior walls at the safe room space with additional steel reinforcement and grout. The safe room is easily completed by adding interior walls constructed of reinforced CMU, a concrete roof deck over the safe room, and a special safe room door, as shown in Figure II-6.

Figure II-5. CMUs were used for the exterior walls at this home under construction (New Smyrna Beach, Florida).

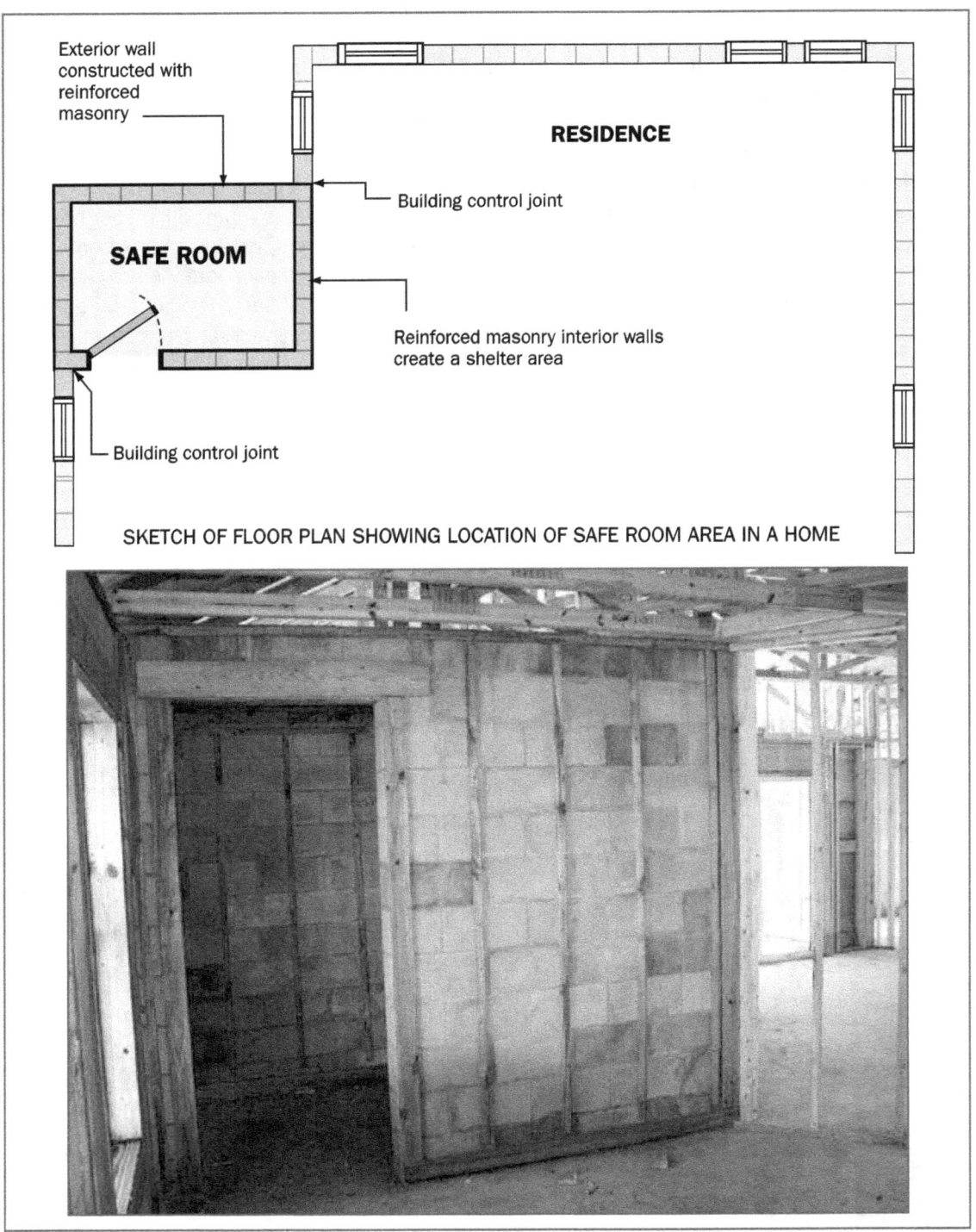

Exterior wall constructed with reinforced masonry

RESIDENCE

Building control joint

SAFE ROOM

Reinforced masonry interior walls create a shelter area

Building control joint

SKETCH OF FLOOR PLAN SHOWING LOCATION OF SAFE ROOM AREA IN A HOME

Figure II-6. View of an in-home safe room under construction. The CMU walls of this safe room are fully grouted and are reinforced, vertically, with steel reinforcing bars from the foundation to the concrete roof deck (New Smyrna Beach, Florida).

Building a safe room in an existing home will typically cost 20 percent more than building the same safe room in a new home under construction. Because the safe room is being used for life safety and your home might be exposed to wind loads and debris impacts it was not designed to resist, an architect or engineer (A/E) should be consulted to address special structural requirements (even when using an A/E in such a project is not required by the local building department).

Safe Room Location

There are several possible locations in your home or small business for a safe room. Perhaps the most convenient and safest is below ground level in your basement. If your home or small business does not have a basement, you can install an in-ground safe room beneath a concrete slab-on-grade foundation or a concrete garage floor. Although basement and in-ground safe rooms provide the highest level of protection against missiles and

Surviving Interior Rooms

falling debris because they may be shielded from direct forces of wind and debris, the above-ground designs provided in this publication are also capable of providing near-absolute protection. This is an important alternative to be aware of if you are not able to install a safe room in your basement due to concerns related to flood hazards or naturally-high groundwater tables at your site.

Another alternative location for your safe room is an interior room on the first floor of the home or small business. Researchers, emergency response personnel, and people cleaning up after tornadoes have often found an interior room of a home or small business still standing when all other above-ground parts of the home or small business have been destroyed. Closets, bathrooms, and small storage rooms offer the advantage of having a function other than providing occasional storm protection. Typically, these rooms have only one door and no windows, which makes them well-suited for conversion to a safe room. Bathrooms have the added advantage of including a water supply and toilet.

Surviving Interior Room

Regardless of where in your home or small business you build your safe room, the walls and ceiling of the safe room must be built so that they will provide near-absolute protection for you, your family, or employees from missiles and falling debris, and remain standing if your home or small business is severely damaged by extreme winds. If sections of your home's or small business' walls are used as safe room walls, those wall sections must be separated from the structure of the home or small business. This is to ensure the structural integrity of the safe room, should the rest of the structure fail or be compromised during an extreme-wind event.

Figures II-7 through II-9 are typical floor plans on which possible locations for safe rooms are shown with yellow highlighting. These are not floor plans developed specifically for homes with safe rooms; they show how safe rooms can be added without changes to the layout of rooms.

Floor Plan 1: basement

Possible safe room locations in a basement include the following:

- In a corner of the basement, preferably where the basement walls are below ground level

- In a bathroom, closet, or other interior room in the basement

- In a freestanding addition to the basement

A space that is to be used for a safe room must be kept free of clutter so that the safe room can be quickly and easily entered and so that the safe room occupants will not be injured by falling objects. For this reason, a bathroom is often a better choice for a safe room than a closet or other space used for storage. Remember, if the basement is below the level of storm surge or the level of flooding from any other source, it is not a suitable location for a safe room. In this situation, a possible alternative would be to build an exterior safe room, adjacent to your home, on a slab-on-grade above the flood level.

Figure II-7.
Floor plan 1: basement

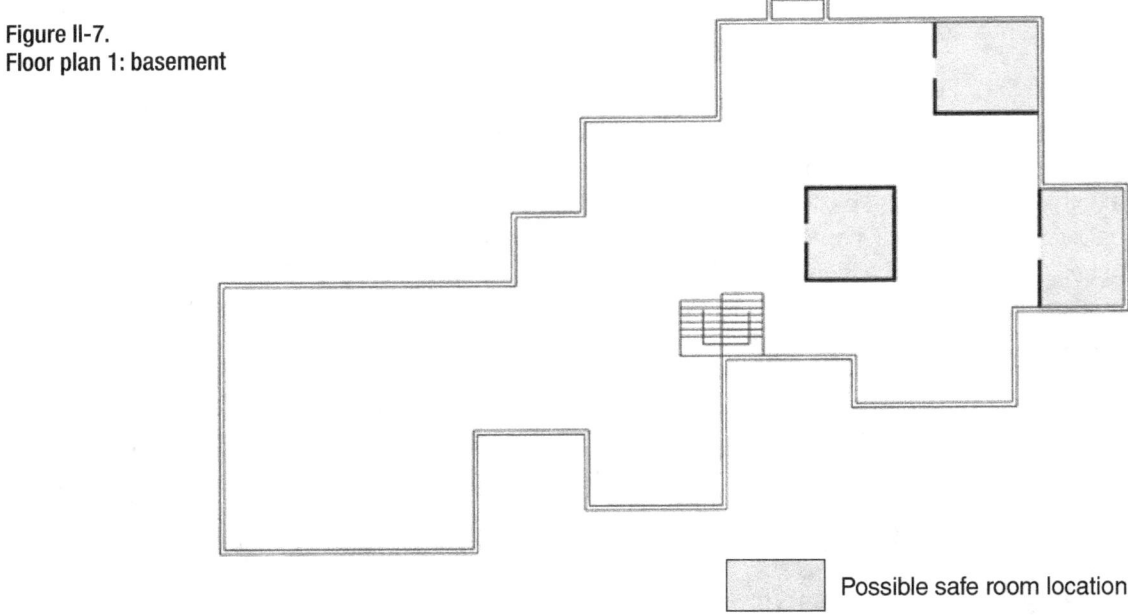

Possible safe room location

Floor Plan 2: safe rooms on the primary level of a home or small business

Possible safe room locations in a home on a slab-on-grade or crawlspace foundation include the following spaces on the first floor:

- Bathroom

- Closet

- Storage room

- Laundry room (provided the load-bearing wall between it and the garage, as shown in Figure II-8, can be properly separated from the structure of the home)

- Corner of the garage

Regardless of where the safe room is built, it must be equipped with a door that will resist the impact of windborne debris (missiles). Remember, if the first floor of the home or small business is in an area that is susceptible to storm surge from a Category 5 hurricane, it is not a suitable location for a residential safe room. Also, installation of safe rooms in SFHAs should only occur if the flood design criteria for FEMA safe rooms are met and approval has been provided by local jurisdictional authorities responsible for evacuating the area in the event of a hurricane and ensuring NFIP compliance. The prescriptive designs presented in this publication can only be elevated a few feet above existing grade and, therefore, may not comply with flood design criteria for residential safe rooms, which means the safe room designs presented in this publication should not be installed. In this situation, a possible alternative would be to build an exterior safe room on a slab-on-grade elevated on fill above the flood level.

Possible safe room location

Figure II-8.
Floor plan 2: home on a slab-on-grade or crawlspace foundation

Floor Plan 3: below-grade safe rooms

Possible locations for an in-ground safe room include the following:

■ Below the slab in a closet or storage room

■ Below the floor of the garage, in an area where cars will not be parked

Because of the difficulty of installing an in-ground safe room in an existing home, this type of safe room is practical only for new construction. Remember, if the first floor of the home is in an area subject to storm surge or below the level of flooding from any other source, it is not a suitable location for a safe room. In this situation, see the previous section for guidance on a possible alternative to build an exterior safe room on a slab-on-grade elevated on fill above the flood level.

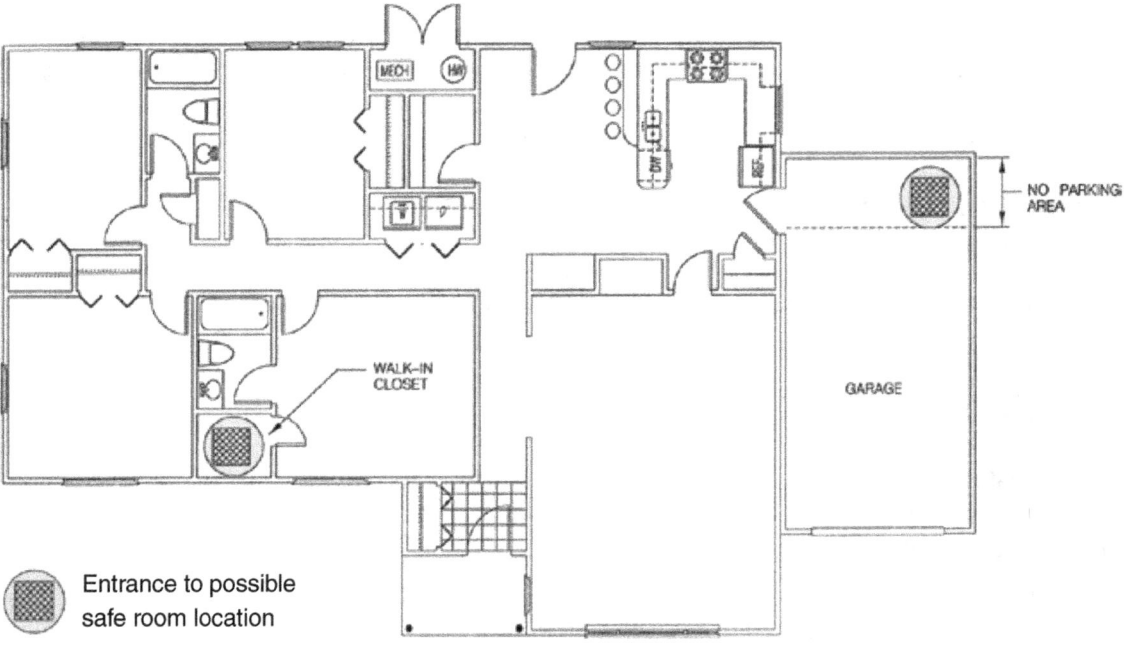

Figure II-9. Floor plan 3: in-ground (below-grade) safe rooms in a home on a slab-on-grade foundation

Floor Plan 4: multi-purpose safe rooms in a small business

Small businesses can use prescriptive safe room designs for multi-purpose safe rooms (see Figure II-10). Using a 14-foot by 14-foot safe room, the area used for life-safety protection can also be adapted for a conference room or other purpose, provided the equipment and fixtures placed in the safe room can be removed quickly and efficiently. When placing safe rooms in buildings larger than typical residential structures, the layout should be designed so that the safe room is quickly accessible from most areas on the floor. If a larger safe room size is desired, design guidance in FEMA 361 can be used.

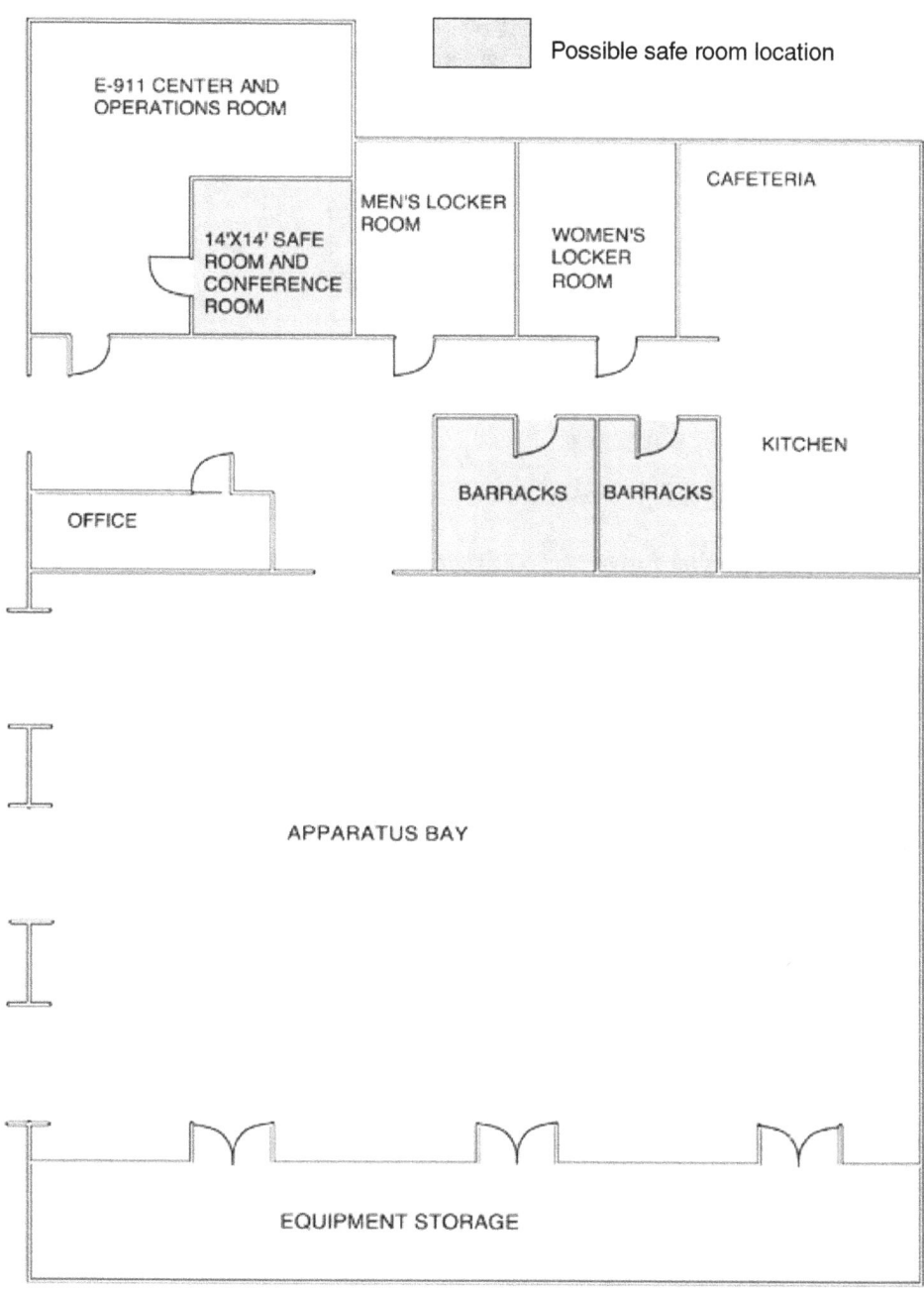

Possible safe room location

Figure II-10. Floor Plan 4: multi-purpose safe rooms in a small business or public building

Tables II-1 and II-2 will help you decide what type of safe room is appropriate for your circumstances. Table II-1 applies to the construction of safe rooms in new homes or buildings. Table II-2 applies to retrofit situations, in which a safe room is being added to an existing home or building.

Table II-1. Appropriate types of safe rooms for new homes and buildings

Safe Room Considerations (New Homes or Buildings)	Appropriate Safe Room Type		
	Basement	In-Ground*	Above-Ground
House or building located in a storm surge area	NA	NA	NA
House or building located in a flood hazard area++	NA	NA	✔
High water table			✔
Low cost	✔		
Long-term safe room occupancy comfort	✔		✔
Least likely to be hit or impacted by windborne debris	✔	✔	

Table II-2. Appropriate types of safe rooms for existing homes and buildings

Safe Room Considerations (Existing Homes or Buildings)	Appropriate Safe Room Type		
	Basement	In-Ground*	Above-Ground
House or building located in a storm surge area	NA	NA	NA
House or building located in a flood hazard area++	NA	NA	✔
High water table			✔
Low cost	✔		
Long-term safe room occupancy comfort	✔		✔
Least likely to be hit or impacted by windborne debris	✔	✔	
Easy retrofit	✔		
Ease of separating safe room from structural framing of house or building	✔	✔	
Minimal disruption to house or building	✔		
Ease of accessibility			✔

NA = Not Appropriate

* The in-ground safe rooms referred to in this publication are built below ground inside a home or building and therefore can be entered directly from within the home or building. Other types of in-ground safe rooms are available that are designed to be installed outside a home or building. Entering one of these exterior in-ground safe rooms would require leaving the home or building. This publication does not contain any designs or other information about exterior in-ground safe rooms.

++ Per flood design criteria for FEMA safe rooms (see pages 23 and 24), elevation of a safe room is only permitted when specific flood design criteria have been met and when approved by the jurisdictional authority responsible for evacuations and NFIP compliance.

Construction Materials

The materials your builder/contractor will need to build your safe room should be available from building material suppliers in your community. These materials have been carefully selected for their strength, durability, and/or ability to be readily combined in ways that enable them to withstand the forces of extreme winds and the impact of windborne missiles. Your builder/contractor should not substitute any other material for those specified in the designs.

One of the most vulnerable parts of your safe room is the door. The WISE Center at Texas Tech University tested the materials specified for doors in the safe room designs in this publication for their ability to carry wind loads and prevent perforation by missiles. The installation of the door is as important as the materials used in its construction. Please confirm with your builder/contractor that the door to your safe room can be installed as shown in the design drawings included with this publication. A door specification has been provided in the plans if you cannot obtain a door that meets the debris impact testing requirements for a 15-lb 2x4 board member traveling horizontally at 100 mph (see ICC-500, Chapter 8 for the debris impact testing procedure to be used).

A complete list of the safe room construction materials, with their expected strengths or properties, is included in the safe room designs provided in this publication. Your builder/contractor should use it when buying the materials for your safe room.

There are other viable and appropriate shelters that have been designed and constructed to meet FEMA's design criteria for residential safe rooms that are not included in this publication. Since the first edition of FEMA 320 was released in 1998, many tornado events have occurred highlighting the importance of installing a safe room in homes or small businesses. Individuals and companies began designing shelters to provide alternatives to the prescriptive solutions presented here. As a result, a residential tornado and hurricane shelter industry has evolved.

Many of these shelter products are designed and constructed as pre-manufactured units. These pre-manufactured units are constructed from a variety of elements such as metal panels, fiberglass shells, Kevlar product systems, and many more. Others are shelters that use common building materials or are new innovations from the building industry such as structural insulated panels (SIPs). Because FEMA 320 was accepted as a "pre-standard" for the design and construction of shelters and safe rooms, many of these shelters have been designed to the FEMA criteria for residential safe rooms; that is, they are capable of resisting 250 mph winds (3-second gust) and the debris associated with such wind events (represented as a 15-lb 2x4 wood board traveling 100 mph).

It is important for prospective safe room owners to know that FEMA does not certify, approve, or license the design and construction of shelters to be

> Structural Insulated Panels (SIPs) are a construction innovation that is being used in some residential construction. SIPs are composite building materials, consisting of two layers of structural board with insulating foam in between.
>
> Some SIPs have been designed such that they are capable of resisting the design wind and debris impact criteria of FEMA 320.

> Additional information regarding pre-manufactured shelters is presented in the Consumer Guide in Section III of this publication. It is important to remember that, as with site-built safe rooms and shelters, pre-manufactured shelters should be attached to an appropriate foundation. A structural engineer should always be consulted to ensure that the pre-fabricated shelter is being installed on an appropriate and adequate foundation.

called safe rooms. However, groups such as the National Storm Shelter Association (NSSA) have stepped forward to help regulate the residential shelter industry. Since the release of its Association Standard in April 2001 (*NSSA Standard for the Design, Construction, and Performance of Storm Shelters*), the NSSA has provided certifications for shelters that meet the FEMA 320 criteria in the form of a quality verification process and seal program. Through independent testing and third party design reviews, participating members of the NSSA have received "seals" indicating that their shelters have been designed to meet the wind and debris impact protection criteria of FEMA 320. As a result, many pre-manufactured shelters have been verified and labeled with "seals" indicating that they comply with the FEMA 320 residential safe room design criteria.

Therefore, when it can be verified that these pre-manufactured shelters are installed on a proper foundation, and are elevated and sited to meet the flood design criteria provided herein, these proprietary shelters can be viewed as an appropriate alternative to the designs presented in this publication.

FEMA supports the work of the NSSA to promote the design and construction of shelters that meet the near-absolute protection criteria set forth in this document. The efforts of NSSA allow individual or proprietary designs to be included in the market place and considered alongside the FEMA safe room designs as options for homeowners and business owners looking to provide protection from extreme-wind events that may impact their homes or buildings. For additional information on the NSSA and other shelter products that meet the FEMA criteria, see the Consumer Guide provided in Section III.

Safe Room Cost

When designed and constructed per the specifications on the design plans, these safe rooms meet or exceed the design requirements for tornadoes and hurricanes as identified in the ICC-500 Storm Shelter Standard. Pre-fabricated shelters are also available for installation by a builder/contractor when first building your home, but are not explicitly addressed by this publication. The basic cost to design and construct a safe room during the construction of a new home starts at approximately $6,000, with larger, more refined, and more comfortable designs costing more than $15,000. The cost of your safe room will vary according to the following:

- The size of the safe room

- The location of the safe room

- The number of exterior home walls used in the construction of the safe room

- The type of door used

- The type of foundation on which your home is built

- Your location within the United States (because of regional variations in labor and material costs)

- Whether you are building a safe room into a new home or retrofitting an existing home

Table II-3 shows the average costs for building two types of safe rooms (above-ground [AG] and in-ground [IG]) in new homes on basement, slab-on-grade, and crawlspace foundations according to the design plans in this publication. These costs are for safe rooms with a floor area of 8 feet by 8 feet and 14 feet by 14 feet.

Table II-3. Average costs for both 8-foot by 8-foot and 14-foot by 14-foot safe rooms in new homes or buildings

Size	Safe Room Type[1,2,3,4]	Applicable Drawing No.	Average Cost[1,3,4]
8-foot x 8-foot x 8-foot Safe Rooms	Concrete Masonry Unit (CMU) Walls	AG-01,02,03	$8,200
	Concrete Walls	AG-01,02,03	$8,100
	Wood-Frame with CMU Infill	AG-05	$7,600
	Wood-Frame with Plywood/Steel Sheathing	AG-06	$6,300
	Insulating Concrete Form	AG-08,09	$8,300
	Reinforced Concrete Box[2]	IG-01	$7,000
14-foot x 14-foot x 8-foot Safe Rooms	CMU Walls	AG-01,02,03	$13,500
	Concrete Walls	AG-01,02,03	$13,100
	Wood-Frame with CMU Infill	AG-05	$13,600
	Wood-Frame with Plywood/Steel Sheathing	AG-06	$11,400
	Insulating Concrete Form	AG-08,09	$13,400

1 All safe room types shown in this table are above-ground (AG) types for slab-on-grade foundations. Safe rooms constructed in basements or on crawlspaces will differ slightly in price based on the foundations used.

2 Below-ground safe room were estimated for a 5-foot by 5-foot by 8-foot (deep) safe room. The cost included a cast-in-place footing and safe room top, but the safe room walls were a pre-cast unit. The costs for these types of safe rooms are very dependent on site-specific soil conditions and the building materials used.

3 See drawings in this publication for specific materials used, sizes, and other values needed for estimating purposes.

4 Costs provided are budgetary cost estimates calculated to 2008 U.S. dollar values.

The cost of retrofitting an existing home to add a safe room will vary with the size of the home and its construction type. In general, safe room costs for existing homes will be approximately 20 percent higher than those shown in Table II-3.

It is also interesting to note that the cost differential between constructing the combined tornado and hurricane safe rooms presented in this publication and those that may be constructed to meet the ICC-500 residential hurricane (only) safe room design criteria is not a significant cost savings. Construction cost comparisons for some of the common building materials used in the prescriptive designs of this publication were performed.

For the masonry and concrete safe rooms, wall and roof sections that were identified through testing as capable of resisting a test missile that had similar impact momentum as the ICC-500 design missile were selected. Because the ICC-500 is a new standard, very few tests have been performed for missile-resistant systems for the ICC-500 missile. Test results from Texas Tech University's WISE Center, Florida A&M University, Florida State University, and the University of Florida were used to identify wall sections that had been tested. For these types of safe rooms, the costs to construct the ICC-500 residential hurricane safe room typically provided a cost savings of only 10 to 15 percent when compared to the cost to construct the FEMA 320 safe rooms presented in Table II-3. Proprietary safe rooms were not included in this cost comparison as no pre-manufactured shelters meeting the new ICC-500 requirements were able to be identified.

These findings, however, were not surprising when considering the common building materials used. As was the case when the First Edition of FEMA 320 was prepared, the safe room design for these small safe rooms is typically governed by the ability of the walls and doors to provide debris impact-resistance. When considering the factors that are involved (250 mph vs. 160 mph design wind speeds and debris impact-resistance for different weight and speed missiles), the net savings is measurable but not large as the reduction of materials from the design is typically limited to a reduction in reinforcing steel, connectors, or wall thickness. For both the masonry and concrete safe rooms, there was still a basic wall thickness that needed to be provided to resist both the debris impacts and the wind loads.

Section III: Building Your Safe Room

Your builder/contractor can use the design drawings provided in this guide to build a safe room for any of the wind zones shown on the map in Figure I-4. The design drawings provided include the details for building five types of safe rooms: concrete, concrete masonry, wood-frame, lean-to, and in-ground. Each of these alternatives is expected to perform equally well in resisting failures caused by extreme winds.

The materials and connections were chosen for their "ultimate strength," which means that the materials are expected to resist the loads imposed on them until they or the connections between them fail. The intent of the designs is not to produce a safe room that will always remain completely undamaged, but rather a safe room that will enable its occupants to survive an extreme windstorm with little or no injuries. The safe room itself may need to be extensively repaired or completely replaced after an extreme-wind event.

The safe room size and materials specified in the drawings are based on principles and practices used by structural engineering professionals and the results of extensive testing for effects of missile impacts and wind pressures. Typical and maximum dimensions have been provided on the drawings. The safe rooms have been evaluated for and comply with the design criteria in FEMA 361 and the shelter standard requirements set forth in the ICC-500 for residential and small community shelters (shelters with less than 16 occupants). Before increasing the safe room size or using material types, sizes, or spacings other than those specified in the drawings, the changes should be reviewed by a licensed professional structural engineer.

The information in this section includes the following:

- Design drawings and details for safe rooms in basements, above the ground, and in the ground
- Designs for safe rooms installed on both slab-on-grade and crawlspace foundations
- General design notes and fastener and hardware schedules
- Materials lists with quantities and specifications

If you or your builder/contractor have questions about the design drawings in this guide, call the FEMA Building Sciences helpline at (866) 222-3580 or email saferoom@dhs.gov for technical guidance.

Index of the Design Drawings

Sheet No.	Drawing No.	Title
1 of 18	T-01	Index Sheet
2 of 18	G-01	General Notes
3 of 18	IG-01	In-Ground Safe Room – Sections and Details
4 of 18	B-01	Basement Lean-To Safe Room
5 of 18	B-02	Basement Safe Room – Corner Location
6 of 18	AG-01	CMU/Concrete Alternative Plans
7 of 18	AG-02	CMU/Concrete Wall Sections
8 of 18	AG-03	CMU/Concrete Sections Ceiling Alternatives
9 of 18	AG-04	Ventilation Details
10 of 18	AG-05	Wood-Frame Safe Room Plan – Plywood Sheathing with CMU Infill
11 of 18	AG-06	Wood-Frame Safe Room Plan – Plywood and Steel Wall Sheathing
12 of 18	AG-07	Wood-Frame Safe Room – Foundation Sections
13 of 18	AG-08	Insulating Concrete Form Plans
14 of 18	AG-09	Insulating Concrete Form Sections
15 of 18	MS-01	Miscellaneous. Details
16 of 18	MS-02	Door Details and Signing Requirements
17 and 18 of 18	ML-01, 02	Materials Lists

* IG = In-ground, B = Basement, AG = Above-ground

How to Use the Drawings

- Drawings should not be scaled to determine dimensions.

- If there is a conflict between a dimension shown on the drawings and a scaled dimension, the dimension shown on the drawing should govern.

- If there is a conflict between the drawings and local codes, the local codes should govern as long as the life-safety protection provided by the safe room is not lessened. It is important to note, however, that the structural, wall, and roof systems should not be compromised because that would reduce the level of protection of the safe room. It is also important to note that these designs exceed most building code requirements.

- If there is a conflict among the general notes, specifications, and plans, the order of precedence is notes, then specifications, then plans.

Consumer Guide

While this guide presents FEMA's guidance on the design and construction of residential safe rooms, FEMA does not test or certify materials or systems used in the construction of safe rooms. Vendor claims of compliance with FEMA and ICC criteria should be verified through independent testing or engineering analysis. The National Storm Shelter Association (NSSA) is a non-profit, industry association dedicated to the storm shelter industry. The NSSA "administers testing and engineering evaluation programs to be conducted by certified, independent entities for the purpose of issuing labels to qualified storm shelter producers." In 2001, the NSSA prepared an association standard for the design and construction of storm shelters. The NSSA Association Standard will be superseded, and the new "Association Standard" will be the ICC-500 Storm Shelter Standard. The NSSA is one place a homeowner or prospective safe room owner can go to seek approved product listings (for safe rooms, shelters, or components) or to verify vendor claims of standards compliance for tornado and hurricane safe rooms.

The NSSA is the only non-profit organization with a quality verification process and seal program. This enables safe room consumers to consider the identity of safe room producers with labeled, quality-verified products; have an industry standard that establishes quality requirements; and be informed and educated on the storm shelter industry via seminars, web pages, and responses to inquiries through the NSSA. The standards to which NSSA holds its manufacturers are consistent with the level of protection provided by the ICC-500 design criteria and FEMA 320. Members of the NSSA that manufacture and construct residential safe rooms submit their designs to the NSSA for third party design reviews to ensure association support for compliance with FEMA 320 and continued respect for the storm shelter industry; it is recommended that all plans used for the construction of safe rooms or shelters be subject to a third party review for quality assurance purposes.

The NSSA website (http://www.nssa.cc) contains a wealth of information such as NSSA policies, evaluation procedures, grant programs, shelter news, and guidance on shelter construction, and industry links. The website also contains contact information for the following different member types:

- **Producer Members** – Those who manufacture or construct storm shelters and certify that shelters, designs, construction, and installation or installation instructions are in compliance with the NSSA standard

- **Installer Members** – Those responsible for compliance with installation instructions provided by producer members

- **Associate Members** – Those engaged in the storm shelter industry, but who do not have direct responsibility for storm shelter compliance with the NSSA standard (this includes suppliers and others engaged in the storm shelter industry)

- **Professional Members** – Design professionals who are capable of designing/analyzing shelters to confirm compliance with applicable standards and other professionals who support the mission of NSSA and also contribute to safety from extreme winds

- **Corporate Sponsors** – Corporate entities with business interests in the storm shelter industry who are willing to support the programs of the NSSA

It is recommended that consumers pursue safe rooms or shelters (manufactured, constructed, or installed) that are per the designs provided in this publication or are verified with a seal from NSSA to meet the FEMA criteria. The NSSA is one place that prospective safe room or shelter owners can look to for verification, certification, and compliance.

Safe Rooms Save Lives

The Oklahoma Safe Room Initiative and rebate program (http://www.gov.ok.gov/display_article. php?article_id=123&article_type=1) built 6,016 safe rooms after the 1999 tornado. There were no deaths during the 2003 tornado that impacted much of the same area also impacted in 1999; the success directly attributable to the availability and utilization of the safe rooms. The Oklahomans in "Tornado Alley" felt safe and protected knowing that their families had a safe place to go. As of March 2008, this and other FEMA grant programs have provided over $260,000,000 in federal funds towards the design and construction of nearly 20,000 residential and over 500 community safe rooms in 23 states and territories.

Below are just a few examples of how FEMA 320 safe rooms have saved the lives of people impacted by extreme-wind events. With proper installation, storm shelters and safe rooms serve as protection from injury or death caused by the dangerous forces of extreme winds. They can also relieve some of the anxiety created by the threat of an oncoming tornado or hurricane. The decision to build or purchase a safe room should include notifying local emergency managers and family members or others outside the immediate area. This will allow emergency personnel to quickly free the exit should it become blocked by debris. For additional information on these and other safe room "success stories," see the FEMA websites listed below.

Baxter County, Arkansas – On February 5, 2008, when a tornado visited the town of Gassville, Arkansas, Jeanann Quattlebaum felt a certain calmness. Less than 10 months prior, she and her husband, Robert, had purchased a storm shelter. The Quattlebaums had been living in their subdivision for seven years. They purchased their home, which was not equipped with a safe room, from an area builder.

Arkansas is one of several states in "Tornado Alley," a term used to describe a broad area of relatively high tornado occurrences in the central United States. The state ranks fourth, after Texas, Oklahoma, and Kansas, with tornadoes that are F3 and higher.

The Arkansas Residential Safe Room Program assists Arkansas homeowners who choose to install a shelter or safe room on their property. The program covers up to 50 percent of the cost and installation, not to exceed $1,000.00, for shelters or safe rooms built on or after January 21, 1999. The Quattlebaums' storm shelter was purchased at a cost of $2,000.00. The circular concrete structure is 10 feet in diameter and stands 5 feet tall. It has the capacity to seat six to eight individuals. During the tornado event of February 5, 2008, it housed six as the tornado touched the lives of Gassville residents. The tornado left behind one fatality and damages to homes and property, which ranged from minimal to extensive.
http://www.fema.gov/mitigationbp/brief.do?mitssId=5466

Oklahoma City, Oklahoma – When Karen and her husband built their retirement home in 2002, they were determined to build a protective safe room equipped with the necessary amenities and materials in the event of a devastating tornado. Instead of building the room inside their home like most people, they decided to construct it 20 feet away from the house, and to build it large enough for their extended family.

"I believe my pets are part of my family," Karen said, referring to her three dogs – two Airedales and a Blue Heeler – and bird – a Scarlet Macaw. "I wasn't going to run three dogs through the house. Because of weather conditions, I couldn't see running three dogs over the carpet." Also, the house was intended to be their last and they wanted it to be a certain way. "It would have been too much structural change," Karen said. "I didn't want to change my basic plans of the house the floor plan I liked. I didn't want to modify it to accommodate everyone."

While the main house is mostly handicapped accessible, it still would have been difficult to construct a safe room inside the house and have someone in a wheelchair enter it without requiring assistance down the stairs. The safe room has a ramp, making it easily accessible for anyone confined to a wheelchair. "It is a retirement home for my husband and I and one of us could end up in a wheelchair someday, [whether] permanently or temporarily," Karen said. "Based on Murphy's Law, that's when a tornado would hit. We just decided to have everything handicapped accessible."

Karen and her husband based their safe room model on FEMA regulations and just added a few additional measures of their own. The room is a reinforced concrete structure with French drains. The front of the cellar faces north and wings are extended on the sides and top to hold back the clay. Four feet of earth also cover the roof of the cellar. Stucco, paint, and water sealer was applied to the concrete and a metal porch was built on top of hickory beams to prevent rain from pouring inside whenever the door was opened. No moisture is likely to leak into the cellar. Karen said she intended to build it that way because she strongly despises a "damp, musty basement."

The project probably cost more than what it normally would have if they had built it inside their home and without all the added weather protection, but Karen was willing to make the sacrifice. She also wanted the room – measured at 10 by 12 feet – to be large enough for her, her husband, and their pets. "I just wanted to take FEMA's requirements [design criteria] and enhance them," she said. "I probably have exceeded their requirements … [so] yes, there was an added expense to have it bigger. But it really didn't add that much. It was worth it to me. That was a personal call. Everybody has to make them."

http://www.fema.gov/mitigationbp/brief.do?mitssId=1345

Autauga County, Alabama – After seeing the destruction of his parents' home, an Autauga County firefighter decided that it is up to him to keep himself and his family safe from storms. Robert Van Valkenburg, 52, decided to look into building a tornado safe room for his home after his parents' home was destroyed by a tornado spawned by Hurricane Andrew. "I grew up in that house and it was lost during Hurricane Andrew, so I take this stuff very seriously," says Van Valkenburg. He adds, "When it impacts your family, and you see how it affects them, you take it seriously and say 'Well if it could happen to my mom and dad, it could happen to me.'"

Van Valkenburg started the process of building his safe room in 2001. He called his local emergency manager and enrolled in the Alabama safe room program sponsored by FEMA and the Alabama Emergency Management Agency. Actual construction of the safe room took place over 8 months in 2002. FEMA paid 75 percent of the cost to build it, $3,500, through its Hazard Mitigation Grant Program (HMGP). "My local emergency managers came out to look at the safe room while it was under construction and took pictures. I had to show an itemized break down of everything, and show the cost to substantiate what I paid for it. Then they gave me the money," Van Valkenburg stated. He also spent more of his own money to add a second entry way to the room, in the event the other entry is blocked, a drainage system, and a generator in the back of his house that kicks in if there is a loss of power.

The safe room got its first test the following spring. Van Valkenburg, his wife, two children, and three dogs stayed in it when a storm system came through and a tornado touched down in the area. "We heard the sirens and went down there in the middle of the night," says Van Valkenburg "I have my pager from the fire department, and when it goes off I know we have severe weather coming into Autauga County. If they say tornado warning we go there." In 2004, his family used the shelter again, but for protection from two hurricanes. Twice during the summer, his family took shelter in their safe room during Hurricanes Ivan and Dennis.

The safe room is 11-by-12 feet and is below the ground under a new wing that Van Valkenburg built onto his house for his elderly father-in-law. It is built to be a natural extension of the house. "I knew because of my wife being claustrophobic, I had to design it where it looked like a room or she wouldn't go into it," he said. The room is made of reinforced concrete and has steel doors that lock from the inside. Van Valkenburg has also equipped it with a big, sturdy bed, battery powered televisions, water, non-perishable foods, a first aid kit, power tools and the negatives to all family photos. "We can come out of there and we can start life again," said Van Valkenburg. "That's what it is all about, coming out of the safe room and being able to live."

http://www.fema.gov/mitigationbp/brief.do?mitssld=1646

Moore, Oklahoma – Don Staley and his family are no strangers to storms and tornados. Their first home was hit by a tornado in October 1998 and suffered minor damage, but was destroyed by another tornado on May 3, 1999. They rode out both storms inside the house. "It was such a frightening sound," he said. "We decided we weren't going to ride out another one inside the house."

In December 2000, the Staleys' new home was ready. Shortly after moving in, they had an above-ground safe room constructed on the back patio. The concrete room has 8-inch thick walls, an 18-inch thick ceiling, a 10-inch foundation, and a sliding entry door made of 12-gauge steel with 3/4-inch plywood on each side. The safe room is equipped with battery-powered lights and a battery-powered television.

When the warning sirens sounded on May 8, 2003, Don took shelter in the safe room along with his dog and two cats to ride out the storm feeling very protected and safe. "I was watching it on TV in there," he recalled. "I could see it was coming my way and I could hear it coming. I could hear the roar. That's a sound you never forget."

When he emerged from the shelter, he found his house in shambles with the roof ripped off. Other houses on the street were also heavily damaged or destroyed. The Staleys used their safe room following the tornado to store and protect belongings they had salvaged. The Stayleys' home was among the more than 300 homes destroyed in the city that day. Whereas a severe tornado hit the city in May 1999 and claimed 44 lives, there were no deaths in the 2003 tornado. The absence of fatalities is being attributed to community preparedness, improved early warning systems, and the many safe rooms and shelters that have been built. Staley sums it all up, "The safe room saved my life, it came through with flying colors. It's worth a million bucks to me."
http://www.fema.gov/mitigationbp/brief.do?mitssId=761

Lowndes County (MS) – North of Columbus, Mississippi is the community of Caledonia. Recently, that town has experienced a bit of growth; folks have moved in and built smaller homes to enjoy a more relaxed country atmosphere. And several United States Air Force retirees have settled there, following a tour of duty at Columbus AFB.

But there have been several storms in that area. In November 2002, a tornado struck and damaged homes and property there as well as other county locations. The State of Mississippi had already recognized the need for storm protection earlier and had instituted a tornado safety program, "A Safe Place to Go". With this declaration, several storm shelter installations were funded by a FEMA Hazard Mitigation Grant. The Wayne Duncan family in Caledonia applied and were reimbursed according to FEMA/MEMA guidelines. An underground safe room was located just outside the carport in the backyard, providing welcome peace of mind.

About 2:00 pm, January 10, 2008, the storm roared across Columbus AFB and a tornado touched down in Caledonia, again. It nearly destroyed the local school, causing damage to several homes. Mrs. Lena Duncan, with her daughter, son-in-law, and the grandbaby, ran from the house into the underground safe room and waited for the winds and rain to stop. The house was heavily damaged, but the family was safe in their shelter.

The Hazard Mitigation Grant Program (HMGP) remains in effect in Mississippi, following the Katrina declaration. Lowndes County is participating in this Grant. This summer, the Duncan family plan to relocate, down the road, in a new home. This new house will be built with a planned inclusion of a safe room, following the guidelines of FEMA 320. Still working in the Lowndes County Courthouse, Lena Duncan encourages anyone who asks about tornado safety to go talk with the Lowndes County Emergency Management officials about tornado preparedness and safety.

One final example discusses the program that funded several of the Oklahoma safe rooms mentioned above:

Oklahoma City, Oklahoma - On May 9, 2003, tornadoes swooped across Oklahoma City's "Tornado Alley." The tornadoes' path was virtually the same as the one that struck 4 years prior. Oklahoma has historically been subject to destructive and deadly tornados and high winds. After the 1999 tornado, 44 persons died, 800 were injured and over 6,000 homes were damaged or destroyed.

In order to make Oklahoma a safer place to live, the state launched a Safe Room Initiative Program. Oklahoma was the first state to promote and implement a Statewide residential safe room initiative to build safer communities. The safe room initiative was implemented by the State of Oklahoma with mitigation funds made available by FEMA through the HMGP. This program funded the building of 6,016 safe rooms across the state.

The three basic objectives to help ensure a successful program were public education, financial assistance, and quality control. First, the State of Oklahoma and FEMA kicked off an extensive Public Education Campaign that encompassed a wide range of outreach projects using public service announcements through radio, television, and print. Books, resources, and educational materials were distributed to the residents and communities, while speakers and meetings were used to reach the general public.

Next, the safe room had to be financially affordable to the people. Federal and State agencies developed a first-in-the-Nation safe room rebate program called "Oklahoma Can Survive" to help cover the cost of constructing safe rooms. A $2,000 rebate was offered to property owners for the building of a safe room [Editorial note: At the time of this program, FEMA estimated the safe room cost of an above-ground safe room was approximately $3,500.] The rebates were given in three phases. Phase 1 provided rebates to those people whose homes were destroyed or substantially damaged in the designated disaster area; Phase 2 provided rebates to people with damaged homes in the designated disaster area; and Phase 3 rebates were provided to anyone in the state who wanted a safe room.

Finally, minimal performance criteria guidelines were enforced for proper safe room construction. FEMA 320 was used as a construction guideline to provide all the information a contractor needed to build a safe room. FEMA then used performance criteria based on FEMA 320. An engineer was retained to assist the state in technical support, and help contractors and educating the general public about choosing a safe room construction contractor and helping homeowners with complaints against contractor performances.

Appendix A: Acknowledgments

The Federal Emergency Management Agency would like to acknowledge the significant contributions made by following individuals in developing the third edition of this publication.

FEMA

John Ingargiola, FEMA Headquarters

Jack Anderson, FEMA Headquarters

Kent Baxter, FEMA Region VI

Marcus Barnes, FEMA Headquarters

Daniel Catlett, FEMA Headquarters

Robert Franke, FEMA Region VII

Edward Laatsch, FEMA Headquarters

John Plisich, FEMA Region IV

Shabbar Saifee, FEMA Headquarters

Jonathan Smith, FEMA Headquarters

Jody Springer, FEMA Headquarters

Keith Turi, FEMA

Zachary Usher, FEMA

Brian Willsey, FEMA

Consultants

Scott Tezak, PE, URS

William Coulbourne, PE, URS

Bill Johnson, URS

Omar Kapur, URS

Bogdan Srdanovic, URS

Deb Daly, Greenhorne & O'Mara

Julie Liptak, Greenhorne & O'Mara

Jimmy Yeung, PhD, PE, Greenhorne & O'Mara

John Squerciati, PE, Dewberry

Wanda Rizer, Consultant

Project Team and Review Committee

Robert Boetler, Mississippi Emergency Management Agency

David Bowman, International Code Council

Ronald Cook, University of Florida

Kenneth Ford, National Association of Home Builders

Dennis Graber, National Concrete Masonry Association

Christopher P. Jones, PE

Ernst Kiesling, PhD, PE, Wind Science and Engineering Center, Texas Tech University

Danny Kilcollins, Florida Department of Emergency Management

Philip Line, American Forestry and Paper Association

Joseph Messersmith, PCA

Tim Reinhold, PhD, Institute for Business and Home Safety

William Rutherford, Clemons-Rutherford

Corey Schultz, PBA Architects, P.A.

Randy Shackelford, PE, Simpson Strong-Tie Company

Larry Tanner, RA, PE, Wind Science and Engineering Center, Texas Tech University

Cliff Vaughn, FlatSafe Tornado Shelters

In addition, FEMA would like to acknowledge the following individuals, who made significant contributions to the October 1998 and March 2004 editions of this publication. (Note: All affiliations were current at the time of publication of the previous editions.)

Design Team

Paul Tertell, PE, FEMA

Clifford Oliver, CEM, CBCP, FEMA

Dr. Ernst Kiesling, PE, Wind Engineering Research Center, Texas Tech University

Dr. Kishor Mehta, PE, Wind Engineering Research Center, Texas Tech University

Russell Carter, EIT, Wind Engineering Research Center, Texas Tech University

William Coulbourne, PE, Greenhorne & O'Mara

Jay Crandell, PE, National Association of Home Builders

Jerry Hoopingarner, National Association of Home Builders

Lionel Lemay, PE, SE, Portland Cement Association

Donn Thompson, AIA, Portland Cement Association

Reviewers

Dennis Lee, FEMA Region VI

Bill Massey, FEMA Region IV

Tim Sheckler, PE, FEMA Headquarters

Dr. Richard Peterson, Department of Geosciences, Texas Tech University

Larry Tanner, RA, PE, Wind Engineering Research Center, Texas Tech University

Richard Carroll, PE, City of Birmingham, Alabama

Brad Douglas, American Forestry and Paper Association

Kenneth Ford, National Association of Home Builders

Richard Vognild, PE, Southern Building Code Congress International